DOING GOOD

Praise For *Doing Good*

'*Doing Good* is a must-read for business leaders across functions. I strongly recommend it as essential reading for Board members as corporate Boards are required to play an increasingly significant role in management of funds for corporate social responsibility. Considering the enormous amount of spend that is going into this area, purely from a business perspective, leaders must read this book so that the money they spend is money well-spent. But as they read the book with that seemingly clinical purpose, they would discover perspective, they would see opportunities, understand the pitfalls, and along the way, many would find the roadmap for a higher calling. *Doing Good* is a much-needed business book. Meena Raghunathan is a deep, lifelong practitioner who has put her real knowledge into this book. Refraining from pontificating, she lends the voice of a sense-maker of a subject that is emerging from the side lines of nice to do, into mainstream corporate strategy.'

—Subroto Bagchi, chairman, Odisha Skill Development Authority and co-founder, Mindtree

'*Doing Good* is a tour de force exposition of the conceptual basis for CSR and the practical aspects of implementing CSR projects. Meena skillfully reinterprets CSR in the relatively more modern setting of TBL (Triple Bottom Line) and fulfillment of SDGs (Sustainable Development Goals) by companies, to convincingly argue that CSR is good for business. Meena then draws on her considerable experience to provide insights into how CSR projects should be designed and executed to maximize the benefits for society.'

—Samir K Barua, former director and professor, Indian Institute of Management–Ahmedabad

‘Finally, a book on the CSR rules in India that is a one-stop repository of all information needed to understand this space. Thanks, Meena, for taking the effort to analyze the complex legislation and write this book. I found the Annexures and the chapter describing the background to how the rules came about to be very useful as well. It’s a must-read book for CSR professionals, NGOs, the government, senior management and Board members.’

—Luis Miranda, chairman and co-founder, Indian School of Public Policy

DOING GOOD

Navigating the CSR Maze in India

Meena Raghunathan

HARPER BUSINESS

An Imprint of HarperCollins *Publishers*

First published in India in English by Harper Business
An imprint of HarperCollins *Publishers* 2022
4th Floor, Tower A, Building No. 10, Phase II, DLF Cyber City,
Gurugram, Haryana – 122002
www.harpercollins.co.in

2 4 6 8 10 9 7 5 3 1

P-ISBN: 978-93-5629-135-5
E-ISBN: 978-93-5629-136-2

Typeset in 10.5/15 Sabon LT Std at
Manipal Technologies Limited, Manipal

Printed and bound at
Thomson Press (India) Ltd

To Barnalee, the colours of joy!

Contents

Foreword

For some years now, the buzz word in corporate circles has been CSR (corporate social responsibility). While it's cousin, ESG, is now competing and drawing a lot of attention, CSR continues to be important, relevant and—of course—(legally) necessary for many companies. The concept of social responsibility has, of course, long been around. Despite the generally prevalent image—especially in India—of businessmen and companies being heartless, greedy and self-serving (further reinforced by their depiction in most commercial films), there are many who are sensitive and contribute to the greater good. Not all sheep are black!

Yet, the popular image of the rapacious businessman—of whom, too, there are innumerable examples—drove the move to *require* corporates to contribute to social and developmental effort. Many felt that mandating this by law was not a good idea. Arguments ranged from this being equivalent to an additional tax burden, to saying it would deprive shareholders from their right to decide how the company profit or their dividend should be used. The political/economic 'Right' opposed it as an unnecessary interference in business (the company's freedom to distribute profits as it chose), while many from the 'Left' opposed it for being a way for the government to shirk its own responsibility by passing it on to the private sector.

Early efforts were limited to 'voluntary guidelines' (which the government brought out in 2009, broadened and updated in 2011), but growing pressure resulted in a law being enacted in 2013. While it made some things—like a Board Committee on CSR—mandatory for large companies, the stipulation of spending 2% of profits (averaged over the last three years) was, in effect, voluntary—there being no enforcement of penalty for non-compliance. The concept was that of 'name and shame', for those who flouted this. New amendments in 2019 brought in penalties—not only monetary but also jail for the person responsible. Further changes in 2021 removed the jail sentences, but continued the monetary penalties.

This book covers all these aspects extensively, providing an excellent history of the evolution of governmental thinking on CSR. To put it in context, it begins with the history of the concept and the academic thinking over the years. It notes that not only the ancient Rig Veda, but every religion advocates giving (Islam has quantified this to the level of the individual). The book notes that SEBI mandated (in 2015) that the large companies also publish a Business Responsibility Report; this has been extended to more companies and its scope broadened (in 2021) to include sustainability. For this, it has defined the format and coverage. Thus, we see the evolution from somewhat fuzzy voluntary guidelines in 2009 to the Triple Bottom Line (people, planet, profits) in 2011 to the legal regimen in 2013 and then its tightening to include penalties for non-compliance.

One major criticism of the CSR law has been that it deals with only 2 per cent of the company's profits. It says nothing about the remaining 98 per cent, nor—more importantly—about how the company makes the profits. This is akin to what I have elsewhere called the 'Tirupati Syndrome': commit all the sins you want, and then absolve yourself by putting a *dakshina* into the *hundi* in Tirupati.

A hypothetical example (which may not be too far from reality) is of a company that voraciously mines ore in forest land, cutting thousands of trees, displacing tribals from their ancestral homes, despoiling the land and polluting the environment. Will a CSR effort—howsoever large—to build schools and health facilities be a recompense? Are such projects a necessary part of development and progress, with the side-effects being assuaged through CSR spends? Are the ill-effects unavoidable 'collateral damage'?

The Business Responsibility and Sustainability Report seeks to address the broader aspects of a company's operations—including how it makes its revenues/profits—but it is moot whether it does so adequately. Many also argue that there are separate laws dealing with the environment, pollution, labour, safety, etc., as also with land acquisition; so, it is unfair to expect that CSR should take care of all aspects. One must admit, if grudgingly, that there is some validity to this argument. That other laws are inadequately enforced, that other regulators are lax in their job, cannot be an argument for putting all the onus on CSR.

As CSR amounts have ballooned (this book estimates the cumulative amount spent to be close to Rs 1,00,000 crore in the six years up to 2019-20), it has become a major source of funds for most NGOs. While many companies have their own Foundations/Trusts, to which much of the required CSR contribution goes, a substantial amount is available for other independent NGOs. With the severe tightening of controls on foreign (FCRA) funding to them, most of these NGOs now look to CSR funds to even continue their operations.

In this context, based on actual experience, there are some problems. One is that the donors—now mainly companies dispensing CSR funds—are driving the agenda of the overall civil society. Thus, because of the preference to fund education (where over a third of CSR funding has gone), NGOs are forced to pivot and focus on this. For the last two years, attention has been on Covid, and while many companies gave generously for this, many other essential tasks and ongoing projects had to be abandoned for lack of financial support.

A second issue is the constant pressure for visible results and on evaluation. Thus, deeper change which takes many years of continuous effort (e.g., regarding the son-preference syndrome or gender discrimination or building cohesive communities), is sacrificed and quick-result, quantifiable-output projects are chosen (number of vaccinations administered, number of toilets built). The reporting and evaluation requirements of CSR regulations have only exacerbated the problem. The emphasis is on 'projects' rather than programmes or processes. Of course, proposals for tribal rights or broader civil rights have no takers.

A new trend (especially in public sector companies) requiring competitive bidding for projects conceived by the corporate, has created other problems. First, the project conceiver (the company) and the implementor (the NGO) are different—not an ideal situation. Second, NGOs are not used to responding to tenders. Many have had to hire someone just to do this. Many tenders allow only a fixed—and inadequate—percentage as overhead, resulting in financial problems for the NGO.

Third, evaluating 'soft' capabilities (commitment, for example) is difficult, especially for corporate managers in the donor company. Finally, there are tax issues regarding GST, about which the rules are ambiguous.

In the last few years, some amount of CSR funds has gone into government programmes like Swachh Bharat and to PM CARES (effectively, to use an oxymoron, a government NGO), putting a strain on NGO finances already under stress because of FCRA regulations. One hopes that corporate donors will again shift focus back to NGOs who have long experience of field work and enjoy a rapport with the intended 'beneficiaries'.

Despite these issues, CSR has been an increasingly important support for NGOs and, more broadly, for various development initiatives, especially in the areas of education and health. In the process, companies and their employees have doubtless developed greater sensitivity to social issues. Even when CSR has been used to indirectly promote brands (and is really as much a marketing spend as a CSR one), the very fact that they pick a certain area (e.g., environment) and blow their horn about the work that they have done, it is an indication of recognising its importance.

Some of these debates about CSR and the seriousness of corporates about it will go on. This book is an important contribution to the very limited authentic literature around CSR, its origins, definitions, concepts, regulations, and practice. It will also serve as a how-to manual for those new to the area, providing useful guidance to companies and to the Board CSR Committees. The author, Meena Raghunathan, has spent decades in work related to critical social needs like skilling, environment and education. Apart from a brief survey of the academic landscape on social responsibility, she brings the reality of field experience and the insights that she has distilled. This book will greatly deepen the understanding of CSR and enrich the discussions around it.

One waits now for another book from Meena which would look at CSR from the perspective of NGOs and provide them with similar insights and guidance. Meanwhile, this book is an invaluable resource and knowledge repository for all those involved (or interested) in CSR.

Kiran Karnik
New Delhi
June 2022

Preface

Corporate Social Responsibility (CSR) is a much-discussed topic in India today—from the boardrooms of corporate India and industry body forums, to government offices, modest NGO premises, and media rooms. While CSR has been practised in the country for a very long time, there has been rising interest in the concept and practice since the enactment of the Companies Act, 2013. Section 135 of the Act (which refers to CSR) has led to a particular interpretation of the subject.

Though the term was coined in the 1950s, we find references in management literature to actions by corporates for the benefit of society since the 1930s. And ever since, its various facets have been controversial. The first major controversy was whether corporates had any business to be in social development at all. The prevailing opinion was best summed up by Milton Friedman's oft-quoted statement, 'The business of business is business.' In his view the only social responsibility of managers was to maximize profits (while adhering strictly to both legal requirements and ethical expectations). Thereafter it was up to the shareholders to donate as they saw fit to social causes (Friedman, 1970).

Since then, academia and the business world have debated various questions around CSR. Is it ethical for managers to divert shareholder money to causes outside the business? Are not corporations taking over government functions and gaining power in matters that they should not have power over? In this process, are corporations not gaining (unjustified) repute? Can the 'good' done in the name of CSR, offset the 'bad' done by polluting or exploitative industries? Can industries get away by patching up the visible ill effects of their actions, without questioning the underlying factors or making any efforts to reform these? Is CSR simply whitewash or greenwash or eyewash?

However, over this course of time, most stakeholders have come to accept that CSR does contribute in some measure to the good of society. Today CSR is an accepted part of doing business. There have been many initiatives, both within CSR and adjacent to it, to make business more responsible and responsive to society and for its responsibilities to be interpreted in a wider sense. And while the older debates continue to remain relevant, a new set of questions has come to the fore.

For instance, is CSR about *doing* good, or is it *being* good? 'Doing good' as in ticking a box by spending a specified percentage of profits? By undertaking community development projects? By being generous, meticulous, well intentioned and professional with regard to spending on these?

Or 'being good' as in a business introspecting and moving its world view from a profit focus to optimizing economic, social and environmental outcomes? Moving from a shareholder perspective to a stakeholder perspective? Making a shift towards business decisions with communities, society, and the environment as core considerations, rather than seeing them as externalities to be managed? From management processes to governance standards?

Is it about how profits are made, or how they are spent?

It is in this context that the law regarding CSR in India has to be viewed. Section 135 of the Companies Act, 2013, made CSR mandatory in India for large companies. The law puts the responsibility of CSR on the company's Board, and lays down processes with regard to setting up CSR Committees, having a CSR policy, and most importantly, spending 2 per cent of the average profit of the last three years on certain types of development projects. It details what constitutes eligible CSR activities, who can implement CSR projects, what geographical areas should be given preference, how CSR activities must be reported, how they must be evaluated, and the consequences of non-compliance.

The law is applicable to a large number of companies—well over 22,000 as of 2019–20—and the general trend is that more are added every year. The law is of interest to NGOs as well, who are often the implementing partners for the corporates.

While the law is a reality, many stakeholders are still coming to grips with issues relating to CSR at conceptual and operational levels. How does one understand a concept which actually has no clear, uniform, and universally accepted definition? About which there are so many debates, discussions and questions, with every stakeholder having their own perspective? How does one contextualize CSR in the framework of larger debates with regard to the ethical, environmental, social, and governance responsibilities of business? How does CSR, as framed by the

Indian law, fit into the larger picture of corporates integrating social and environmental concerns into their core business? How does one understand a term like CSR which is related to so many other management terms and concepts? And how does one begin to operationalize a law which is largely without precedent anywhere in the world? One which is constantly evolving and changing? Where compliance requirements are becoming more and more complex, time-consuming, and stringent?

This book hopes to provide a background to help readers do some of this. It is as much a result of having been a CSR practitioner for fifteen years, having seen CSR operations in India before and after the Act, and having a boardroom perspective on it, as from being a student of CSR and therefore studying it from an academic perspective.

Hopefully, it answers more questions than it raises!

1
Understanding the CSR Landscape

How strange to begin a book on Corporate Social Responsibility by stating that there is no clear, unambiguous, and universally-accepted definition of the term! And that too for a concept that is not new, and that in recent years has become the subject of everyday conversation—at least in India. When we say that the concept of CSR is not new, what exactly do we mean? Well, CSR has been discussed in management literature since the 1930s and '40s. But the practice goes much further back than that. Businesses have, through the ages, been contributing to social welfare, and references to such contributions can be traced back for centuries.

Traditionally, these contributions were in the form of donations and charities for causes that touched the hearts of the owners. The period around the mid-1800s saw a paradigm shift in the wake of the first industrial revolution. Businesses launched welfare efforts for the safety and well-being of the workforce. Whether this was out of a sense of responsibility or to achieve greater productivity, or both, is not clear. Whatever the motivation, there were significant initiatives to improve conditions in factories as well as living conditions of workers. Among those industrialists were some who were truly enlightened, whose vision and thinking were far ahead of the times, propelled by deep and genuine concern for workers and their rights. One such was Jamsetji Tata (see Box 1.1).

Box 1.1: The Vision of Jamsetji Tata

A pioneer in setting India on the path to industrial self-reliance, Jamsetji Tata did not only introduce new technologies and machinery. As far back as in the 1880s he offered facilities like crèches for workers in his mills, as well as decent working hours, properly ventilated workspaces, fire safety, etc. In 1886 he instituted a Pension Fund, and in 1895, began to pay accident compensation. His vision for the well-being of his workers was truly enlightened.

The story of Jamshedpur is another testimony to his vision. The work on this township for housing the workers of the steel mills commenced in 1908. More than just basic housing for his workers, he wanted to build a proper modern planned city. His instructions were: 'Be sure to lay wide streets planted with shady trees, every other of a quick-growing variety. Be sure that there is plenty of space for lawns and gardens; reserve large areas for football, hockey and parks; earmark areas for Hindu temples, Muslim mosques and Christian churches.'

Based on: https://www.tatasteel.com/media/6085/jamshedpur-brochure.pdf and www.tata.com

Defining CSR: A Problematic Issue

From the very start of the CSR journey, the understanding of the term and the scope and scale of activities have been constantly evolving. But consensus on a definition of CSR is yet to be reached!

It was in the 1930s and '40s that academic literature began discussing the social responsibilities of business in a broader context. Formal definitions and frameworks of CSR started evolving around the 1950s. The term 'Corporate Social Responsibility' itself was coined in 1953 by American economist Howard Bowen in his book *Social Responsibilities of the Businessman*. Since then, the scope of the term has been expanding and evolving and it now encompasses the understanding that businesses have a responsibility to all stakeholders, not just shareholders; and that social responsibility includes ethics and good governance.

Through the decades, many academics, practitioners, policymakers, and institutions have given their own definitions, but not one of these is universally agreed upon or used. The understanding of CSR differs from country to country, from decade to decade, company to company, and stakeholder to stakeholder. Due to the multiplicity of definitions, many have taken the view that CSR is very loosely or subjectively defined, to the extent that the definitions are not very meaningful. Peter Frankental (2001) of Amnesty International goes to the extent of saying 'CSR is a vague and intangible term which can mean anything to anyone, and is therefore effectively without meaning.'

What shall we do under the circumstances? How shall we define or even get a sense of what CSR is? Maybe instead of looking at one definition, we can look at several popular ones, and readers can construct their own understanding and definition.

So here goes, with a sample list of definitions that would give an idea of what CSR has meant to different people at different times. Definitions given by eminent thinkers (going by the author's own preferences) starting from the 1950s, provide a flavour of the evolution of the term. Howard Bowen (1953), considered by many to be the Father of CSR, defined it as follows: 'It (Social Responsibility) refers to the obligations of businessmen to pursue those policies, to make those decisions, or to follow those lines of action which are desirable in terms of the objectives and values of our society.'

Prominent business thinker William Frederick (1960) put it thus: 'Social responsibility in the final analysis implies a public posture towards society's economic and human resources and a willingness to see that these resources are utilized for broad social ends and not simply for the narrowly circumscribed interests for private persons and groups.'

A point to note in these early definitions is that they recognize that business has a responsibility to society, but leave the decision of what is socially responsible to the corporate entities.

Archie Carroll (1979), a renowned academic who has done much work in this area, said: 'The social responsibility of business encompasses the economic, legal, ethical, and discretionary expectations that society has of organizations at a given point in time.' His 'CSR Pyramid' is a foundational framework in conceptualizing CSR, in terms of the Economic, Legal, Ethical and Philanthropic responsibilities of business. Thomas Jones (1980) defined CSR as 'the notion that corporates have an obligation to constituent groups in society other than stockholders and beyond that prescribed by the law and union contract'.

In these two definitions, we see a movement towards social responsibility as an obligation and a requirement. Seen as a legitimate expectation of society over and above the law, they widen the focus of the business from shareholders to stakeholders.

Moving to the next decade, Frederick et al. (1992) defined CSR as 'a principle stating that corporates should be accountable for the effect of any of their actions on their community and environment'.

Then we come to the definition of CSR given by Jorg Andriof et al. (2002): 'recognition that day-to-day operating practices affect stakeholders and that is in those impacts where responsibility lies, not merely in efforts to do good'.

Werther and Chandler (2011) move the needle with their focus on strategic CSR, which they define as 'The incorporation of a holistic CSR perspective within a firm's strategic planning and core operations so that the firm is managed in the interests of a broad set of stakeholders to achieve maximum economic and social value over the medium to long term'.

These definitions give the broad conceptual framework in which CSR is now understood—the business–society interface. They imply that in such a web, business cannot undertake actions which go against the interests of larger society. They stress on the concept of accountability and explicitly refer to the responsibilities of business towards the community and the environment. These authors and thinkers leave no doubt that CSR is responsible business practice, and not philanthropy, charity, or social welfare.

However, most of the definitions above are from academics. How do international organizations articulate their perspectives on CSR?

Key Institutional Definitions

In 2000 World Business Council for Sustainable Development defined CSR as 'The continuing commitment by business to behave ethically and contribute to economic development while improving the quality of life of the workforce and their families as well as of the local community and society at large'.

The European Union (EU) defines CSR as 'the responsibility of enterprises for their impact on society', and mentions that it can be met by companies through 'integrating social, environmental, ethical, consumer, and human rights concerns into their business strategy and operations' and by 'following the law' (ec.europa.eu).

According to the United Nations Industrial Development Organization (UNIDO) website:

> Corporate Social Responsibility is a management concept whereby companies integrate social and environmental concerns in their business operations and interactions with their stakeholders. CSR is generally understood as being the way through which a company achieves a balance of economic, environmental and social imperatives ('Triple-Bottom-Line Approach'), while at the same time addressing the expectations of shareholders and stakeholders.
>
> (www.unido.org)

Several facets of social responsibility come out of these definitions: the need to follow the rule of law, ethical behaviour, and going above and beyond legal requirements. The need to integrate environmental and social concerns into business planning and operations is stressed so that CSR is the way in which business is done, and not an add-on. Businesses are urged to take responsibility for their actions, and to contribute to economic development and quality of life.

Incidentally, some scholars have also proposed the concept of 'Corporate Social Irresponsibility' or CSI (see Box 1.2).

Box 1.2: Corporate Social Irresponsibility!

A concept linked to CSR is CSI—Corporate Social Irresponsibility. This too has several definitions.

J. Scott Armstrong (1977) defines CSI as follows: 'A socially irresponsible act is a decision to accept an alternative that is thought by the decision maker to be inferior to another alternative when the effects upon all parties are considered.'

Matthew Kotchen and Jon Moon (2012) state: 'Corporate social irresponsibility is a set of actions that increases externalized costs and/or promotes distributional conflicts.'

Nick Lin-Hi and Karsten Müller (2013) note: 'Another way to look at it (CSI) is to contrast it to CSR which is usually understood as "doing good". But corporations also have the responsibility for "avoiding bad" in order to prevent Corporate Social Irresponsibility (CSI), such as cheating customers, violating human rights, or damaging the environment.'

A Distillation

An analysis by an academic, Alexander Dahlsrud (2006), may help us crystallize the core elements of CSR. He decided to statistically examine thirty-seven widely-used definitions of CSR. Through this, he found five widely prevalent threads or dimensions across the definitions: the Stakeholder dimension, the Social dimension, the Economic dimension, the Voluntariness dimension, and the Environmental dimension. He makes the point that 'none of these definitions actually defines the social responsibility of business'. Rather, they 'describe CSR as a phenomenon' (ibid.).

And while India is one of the first countries to mandate CSR, the section that discusses CSR—Section 135 of the Companies Act, 2013—does not actually define it!

Even though there is no clear answer to the question 'What is CSR?', readers must by now have formed some idea of what it means or ought to mean. Each forthcoming decade and each country will continue to define CSR for itself. This understanding of CSR will be significantly impacted by current events—for instance, a major pollution incident or a pandemic like Covid would reshape the understanding of business–society interaction. The understanding of CSR will also be influenced by evolving norms and standards of governance and business ethics. But one thing is certain, the world is unlikely to go back from the understanding that business has to be aware of and responsible for its actions and the impact of these actions on the rest of society.

Charity, Philanthropy and CSR

We will, through the course of the book get glimpses of the various facets of CSR, and also see how the understanding of

CSR in India relates to the universal understanding of the concept of CSR. Scholars today agree that CSR is responsible business practice, and that it is not philanthropy or charity. At this stage, it would be helpful to pause and quickly review the terms 'charity' and 'philanthropy', and distinguish them both from CSR.

The 'giving' impulse is as old as humankind. Every religion advocates it, and every society has practised it down history. Historically, charity and philanthropy have generally been driven by religion. Charity attempts to eliminate suffering caused by social problems; while philanthropy—derived from the Greek words 'philos' (love) and 'anthropos' (humankind) and thus roughly translating to 'love for humankind'—tries to solve the social problems which cause suffering. For instance, a donation to feed the hungry is charity. A programme to help the hungry to learn a skill and fend for themselves is philanthropy.

So charity is like treating symptoms without worrying about the disease itself, whereas philanthropy tries to diagnose the disease and treat it. Philanthropy has played a very important role in society. Often it has supported the setting up of institutions which benefit us all—from hospitals to scientific institutions to universities to libraries. The Indian Institute of Science (IISc), for instance, is an outcome of philanthropy, as is the Birla Institute of Technology and Science (BITS) in Pilani (see Box 1.3).

Box 1.3: From Temples to Gods, to Temples of Education

G.D. Birla was at the forefront of nation building. He was a strong supporter of Gandhiji and gave considerable support to the freedom struggle.

Many of us would have at some time or other visited a Birla Mandir—many a large town in India boasts one.

> Apart from this charitable activity of temple building, a landmark contribution of the Birlas is the creation of one of India's best higher educational institutions—the Birla Institute of Technology and Science (BITS).
>
> This was started as a school for G.D. Birla and R.D. Birla by their grandfather in 1901. It grew into a high school in the 1920s. In the '40s, the Birla Education Trust was founded and the institution went from strength to strength, adding degree and postgraduate courses in a variety of disciplines. In 1964, taking advantage of a Ford Foundation grant, the institute formed a partnership with Massachusetts Institute of Technology (MIT), USA, and was well on the path to leading India's achievements in technical education.
>
> Based on https://bits-pilani.ac.in/bitsFactsHistory

Philanthropists are people who use their own wealth and therefore may deploy it as they please for the causes of their choosing, in the manner of their choosing. This is a double-edged sword. On one hand, this enables them to take up causes which may at that time be unpopular or controversial and therefore do not have the support of the public or the government. But the lack of accountability in giving is not without its risks.

In the mid-1980s, it was private foundations that led the charge against AIDS, a risky subject at that time about which governments were not doing much. Private philanthropy contributed substantial financial resources to the cause, which helped lay the foundation for testing, research, and prevention. Similarly, Indian industrialists of the early nineteenth century contributed significantly from their personal wealth towards India's freedom struggle.

However, lack of accountability comes with risk. Very large philanthropic donations may have a significant impact at the national level—either by setting up parallel systems outside public scrutiny or by changing national priorities. For instance, during the Covid pandemic, suppose a private foundation bestowed huge grants on research institutions to fund research on a particular line of vaccine. Recipient institutions—especially if cash-strapped—would focus their resources on this line of research due to the resources made available, rather than one that they might have considered more desirable.

In fact Chuck Collins and Helen Flannery (2016) have noted: 'Unchecked, private foundations can become blocks of concentrated unaccountable power with considerable clout in shaping our culture. They can become extensions of personal power, privilege, and influence for a handful of wealthy families.'

Philanthropy and CSR are often misconstrued as being synonymous. However, there is a significant difference between them. Philanthropy is defined as promoting and attempting to bring about social change by making generous financial contributions. Philanthropists are people who want to contribute money, time or knowledge for a cause that they believe in. It is not just individuals who are philanthropic. Companies too can make philanthropic contributions or donations to causes they believe in. They may or may not be closely involved in the activity itself, though of course they would like to track the impacts and outcomes the contribution has.

On the other hand, CSR goes beyond that. A holistic universal understanding of CSR is that it is about making the core business functions of a company more sustainable so as to benefit both the community and also the business; and widen the focus of business to include concern for all stakeholders, rather than just shareholders. It is about bringing in better governance. Philanthropic work of a company does not require it to change its business practice. However, CSR might need a company to change certain important business practices in order to make itself a more responsible business.

In India, there are several business leaders who distinguish clearly between personal philanthropy and company CSR (also see Box 1.4). To quote just one example, the Azim Premji Foundation which works at scale on Education across the country, as per its website, 'is funded solely by Azim Premji by way of transfer of his personal shares in Wipro to the Foundation'; while Wipro Foundation is the CSR arm of Wipro (azimpremjifoundation.org).

Box 1.4: The Giving Pledge

The Giving Pledge is a commitment by the world's wealthiest individuals and families to dedicate a majority of their wealth to giving back to causes of their choice, either in their lifetimes or through their wills. Initiated by Bill and Melinda Gates and Warren Buffett in 2010, as of 2020, there were 210 people and families who had taken this pledge. Azim Premji was the first Indian to commit himself to this. Kiran Mazumdar-Shaw, Rohini and Nandan Nilekani are among the others.

Based on https://givingpledge.org/

Not just the extremely wealthy, even the middle classes in India are committing to giving back. The 'Living My Promise' is a pledge many are taking, to 'give back at least 50% of my wealth to charitable causes of my choice while I am alive or in my will'.

www.livingmypromise.org/

As we shall see, the core requirement of the Companies Act, 2013, in India is that large companies spend a certain percentage of profits on community programmes. If a company feels it is fulfilling its CSR responsibility by carrying out programmes as mandated under the Act, however well structured, well implemented, and impactful these programmes are, it is meeting the letter of the law, but not the spirit of CSR. To meet the spirit, it must also look inwards into its business practices and make changes there.

Factors that Shape CSR

We have seen the 'giving' impulse which has historically been at the root of CSR, and the ethical reasons which are increasingly becoming significant. There are also several business reasons that drive companies to undertake CSR—from the need for social license to operate, to risk mitigation. But what actually shapes the CSR that a company does? At a broad level, there is an interplay of many factors which gives shape to how it views and undertakes CSR. These factors can be largely clubbed under two heads: external (to the company), and internal (or firm-level) factors.

External factors

These cover the larger environment in which the business exists. Philanthropy and CSR are strongly influenced by the specific and unique history, culture, ethics, and social traditions as well as by the economic and political organization of the society in which they exist.

How does a country's economic system affect CSR? Some scholars opine that CSR activities are essentially a way of redistributing funds from firms to the public, and hence CSR is likely to be significantly determined by the prevalent political climate and context, for instance, whether a company is operating in a strongly capitalistic society or a socialistic one, etc. The overall state of the economy has significant impacts on the scope, shape and size of CSR. In recent decades, as economic and ethical crises have shifted the priority of stakeholders from high economic growth to inclusive growth, CSR has become even more important.

How do social and cultural factors affect CSR? For instance in India, people do not talk about their charitable actions, donations, etc. Some scholars opine that this has carried over into CSR as well, and that is why historically, though CSR has been widely practised in India, its magnitude has not been publicized in proportion.

How does the legal environment in India affect CSR? India is among the few nations in the world that has a law on it. Who needs to do CSR, how they need to do it, and what they can do, etc., are all laid down in the law. Even companies with a long history of CSR have tweaked or changed their priorities, implementation strategies, etc., in response to this law that came into force in 2014.

Among other factors driving CSR we could also include factors such as the sector to which a company belongs (and therefore the impact of the company on the environment and society); consumer pressure for responsibly made products and better environmental and social performance; NGO challenges to corporate reputations; codes of conduct for industry associations; the prevalence of CSR performance ratings and rankings; and importantly, investor demands.

Internal factors

This second set of factors may be called 'firm-level factors' that influence or drive CSR. These include the size and scale at which the firm operates; whether it is multinational or domestic; risk mitigation; cost management (including tax saving); managing its visibility in the public eye by enhancing the positive perception of the company in the eyes of various stakeholders, including via brand building; and attracting, training and retaining of employees. All these factors are significant internal drivers of a firm's social and environmental initiatives.

In addition, in India where family-owned firms traditionally dominate, a strong internal driver for CSR has been the founder's personal convictions and desire to contribute to society's development, a form of 'giving back'. Spirituality or religious beliefs of business owners continue to influence CSR in India to date.

Enlightened self-interest, driven by the need and desire of corporates to seek legitimacy, may also be an underlying driver for CSR. This usually takes the form of strategic CSR, when there are clear benefits to the firm from taking these actions.

Sometimes, it is the fear of government regulations that drives CSR. At other times, the conclusion that the government is not able to adequately address social and environmental challenges results in the decision by the corporates to step in.

The CSR of a firm is thus usually shaped by a complex interplay of these external and internal factors.

Criticisms against CSR

An understanding of CSR would not be complete without understanding the criticisms levelled against it. Indeed, CSR has been and remains a controversial topic. Naysayers have criticized CSR from various angles. One of the first to do this way back in 1958 was Harvard economist Theodore Levitt who said that 'government's job is not business, and business's job is not government'.

Milton Friedman (1970) was one of the people who consistently opposed CSR from a business point of view. He opined that it would be most dangerous to accept that business has, 'a social responsibility that goes beyond making as much as possible for their shareholders'. His article in the *New York Times* implies that CSR is, in fact, an immoral business practice because corporations spend the money of shareholders on social causes without their consent. He continued to hold and build on this theme through the years.

Apart from this school of criticism with regard to resource 'mis-allocation', there are several other schools of criticism. The most important may be that philanthropic activities can be used to hide unscrupulous business actions. Many scholars worry that firms may ignore responsible principles of production of wealth and then become generous in distributing this wealth in the name of philanthropy or CSR. They argue that CSR takes away the spotlight from how businesses operate, how they make their wealth, and tries to refocus the spotlight on how they spend a small part of these profits.

In many cases CSR is also dismissed as greenwashing—a term which implies the 'selective disclosure of positive information about a firm's environmental or social performance, while withholding negative information on these dimensions' (Lyon and Maxwell, 2011).

There are many who argue that CSR does not address the underlying structural conflicts between a company and its stakeholders, ignores poverty and resource-use impacts of business activities, and hence does not address the core of the problem. Also, CSR is viewed suspiciously because it leaves out critical issues (for instance, tax avoidance or abuse of market power), from the mainstream of discussions.

Some see CSR as an attempt by governments to disown their responsibility for the provision of public goods, moving the responsibility to corporations.

There is also an apprehension that through CSR, large corporates may exert increasing influence in public-policy processes through partnerships, consultations, participation, etc. As per Bryane Michael (2003), CSR makes it possible for corporates to jostle 'for the right to determine social objectives and the funding of these objectives'. He opines that by allowing corporates to decide CSR priorities, it 'offers policymaking powers to businesses' (ibid.). These critics see it as a way for corporates to go beyond their mandates and not only step into spheres where they should not be acting, but also using it as a way to gain undue legitimacy in areas which should be the prerogative of democratically elected governments. Gerard Hanlon and Peter Fleming (2009) have gone so far as to term CSR, 'a predatory soft power form of extending corporate influence'.

There are many who believe that companies undertake CSR primarily as a public relations (PR) exercise; that they embrace CSR enthusiastically because it gives them a good image with various stakeholders, thus attracting customers, talent, investors, and general goodwill.

Critics also posit that firms undertake CSR to provide reassurance to the government that they are voluntarily doing something about environmental or societal concerns, hence preventing legislation or regulation which will force them to make more fundamental changes in the way they work. In an even worse case, they may use CSR to take away focus of the powers-that-be from some of their less acceptable activities.

Some argue that CSR can be a means for unscrupulous firms to eliminate competition by pretending to undertake CSR on a large scale in the short term so that more scrupulous firms, which do not want to do things just for show, appear at a disadvantage in the eyes of various stakeholders.

CSR has also been criticized for misguiding potential employees. It is alleged that some companies present themselves as more attractive employers by highlighting their CSR. It is also sometimes cynically said that CSR positioning of a company provides an easy way out for young people who want to earn well by joining corporations that stamp themselves as doing good CSR.

The concept has also come under fire because some feel that it is overly focused on 'management, measurement and metrics' rather than on sensitivity to real social issues, social processes, and nuances.

Another criticism put forward by Porter and Kramer (2006) states: 'Frequently ... CSR efforts are counterproductive, for two reasons. First, they pit business against society, when in reality the two are interdependent. Second, they pressure companies to think of corporate social responsibility in generic ways instead of in the way most appropriate to their individual strategies.'

In the Indian context, a relevant fear is that CSR may give a false sense of comfort to businesses. They may conclude that by spending some part of their profit on CSR activities they are not only compliant but have also discharged their societal responsibilities, whereas the real need is for corporations to be more accountable as to how they conduct business and make profits. The latter part of the criticism by Porter and Kramer—of pushing companies to think in 'generic ways' rather than in a company-specific strategic way—may also be something that may be happening, thanks to the law providing a menu of causes for companies to take up, rather than encouraging them to tailor-make material, holistic programmes which respond to the needs of their stakeholders.

2

Exploring the Larger Context

Anyone working in CSR will encounter a plethora of related terms and concepts. It is sometimes difficult to unravel the linkages: Are they identical, related or adjacent? How are they related? Which term encompasses which other term? Which is wider in scope?

Keeping this in mind, here is an introduction to some terms, concepts and approaches that often come up in CSR-related discussions. Each is a field on its own, and what is provided here is only a glimpse to serve as an introduction for CSR practitioners. Most of these concepts are not fundamentally different in their vision or goals—rather they are different approaches with different emphases. Some readers may want to read the chapter in detail. For others, I would suggest you skim through it to become familiar with the terms. You can always return to this section when you want to follow any of these approaches—you will know where to get a basic introduction.

The Triple Bottom Line

Traditionally, we think of profits being the bottom line that defines the success or failure of a business. Conventionally, textbooks on business management once defined the only objective of a business being the maximization of value for the shareholder. As long as they were within the law, the received wisdom was that they need not worry about anything else. However, since the mid-1990s—with the world becoming increasingly frustrated by the negative impacts of businesses on the environment and on communities—it began to be recognized that the objective of a business could not simply stop at generating profits for its shareholders, who were after all just one set of stakeholders.

Introduced by John Elkington in 1994, the paradigm of Triple Bottom Line (TBL) is summed up as the 3P approach—paying attention to Profit, People and Planet. The TBL is an accounting framework which takes into consideration all three parameters. Apart from measuring profit, it also measures the impact of the business on the environment and society. Looking at the 3Ps in a little more detail will help us understand what TBL must take into account.

'People' refers to the impact that the business has on all the people who are stakeholders of the company—from employees, vendors, and customers, to the community and anyone else impacted by the organization. Paying attention to the People dimension includes a focus on fair and non-exploitative labour practices, employee diversity, investing in workforce health, safety, well-being, development, etc. It would also take into consideration the impact of the organization's operations and products on customers. At the same time, it would need the organization to look outwards, ensuring that the immediate community, as well as society at large, would not be negatively impacted. On the contrary, it would need the organization to contribute positively by investing in the community.

The Planet dimension refers to the actions and impacts of the organization on the environment. In order to improve this dimension, organizations need to work towards reducing their ecological footprint—in other words, reducing the negative impacts their activities have on the environment. Such actions could range from decreasing emissions, effluents, noise, energy and resource consumption, moving to renewable energy, etc. Organizations need to be mindful of their exploitation of the environment as a source of raw materials, and of their use of it as a sink for emissions and other forms of pollution. With the world taking on targets for carbon neutrality and zero emissions, these become actionable goals for organizations to work towards.

The Profit dimension is one that businesses are well aware of, and it needs no elaboration here!

The TBL approach seeks to optimize all three objectives (profit, people, planet), and not maximize one at the cost of the others—for example, maximizing profits for shareholders by exploiting labour.

Of course it is not easy to balance the Triple Bottom Line. Even if managements are convinced of the importance of doing this and are committed to the approach, there are many operational problems. To begin with, how are benefits to the environment and society to be measured and quantified? There is no formula to do this! Also, environmental and social impacts are long-term and may not readily fit into a financial-year (FY) approach. While there are several approaches each with their strengths and weaknesses, proponents and opponents, there is no uniform and standardized method as of now. One approach is to monetize all dimensions of the TBL and state all costs and benefits in monetary terms. But this monetization of different dimensions is a subjective exercise. Another approach is to put TBL in terms of an index, which is then used to compare 3P performance between comparable entities.

While TBL aims to measure the financial, social, and environmental performance of a company over time, and is a useful way of measuring and reporting a company's efforts towards sustainability and CSR, it must be borne in mind that there is still some way to go in operationalizing this in a universally applicable way.

Box 2.1: Blended Value

Disucussing the Blended Value theory, Jed Emerson (2010) states that 'value itself is whole and nondivisible'. In this paradigm, it is posited that organizational value is created by 'the interaction over time of three primary value components: social, economic, and environmental'.

In this framework, the assessment of an organization depends on the value it creates, keeping in mind financial, social and environmental values.

Responsible Business

Responsible business and TBL are close in that underlying both is the principle that a business cannot focus on profit alone, and it is not enough to maximize returns to shareholders. A business needs to optimize gains for all stakeholders, through focusing not just on profits, but giving due importance to people and the planet also.

Compared to TBL, responsible business has a significant additional dimension—that of ethics. While most definitions of

CSR and related terms do not have an explicit reference to ethical conduct, responsible business is explicitly concerned with *how* business is done, in other words, the ethics of the organization.

Responsible business goes beyond how an organization carries on its *own* business. This involves taking responsibility for its actions in the widest sense—for instance, labour practices in its suppliers' factories. A responsible business would need to take a variety of actions in its quest towards responsible business practices, not only within the organization but also through the supply chains and across the product life cycle.

The wide scope of the concept can be seen from the reporting formats used for measuring a business based on this approach. For instance, the Securities and Exchange Board of India (SEBI) mandated in 2015 that the largest companies in India report their performance with regard to responsible business covering nine principles. Previously called Business Responsibility Reporting, the formats have been updated in 2021, and the report is now called the Business Responsibility and Sustainability Report. The nine principles—articulated in 2019 by the Ministry of Corporate Affairs as the National Guidelines on Responsible Business Conduct—are:

Principle 1: Businesses should conduct and govern themselves with integrity and in a manner that is ethical, transparent, and accountable.

Principle 2: Businesses should provide goods and services in a manner that is sustainable and safe.

Principle 3: Businesses should respect and promote the well-being of all employees, including those in their value chains.

Principle 4: Businesses should respect the interests of and be responsive to all its stakeholders.

Principle 5: Businesses should respect and promote human rights.

Principle 6: Businesses should respect and make efforts to protect and restore the environment.

Principle 7: Businesses, when engaging in influencing public and regulatory policy, should do so in a manner that is responsible and transparent.

Principle 8: Businesses should promote inclusive growth and equitable development.

Principle 9: Businesses should engage with and provide value to their consumers in a responsible manner.

(In the context of human rights, it would also be useful to refer to the UN's Guiding Principles on Business and Human Rights.)

Box 2.2: Corporate Citizenship

According to Adam Hayes (2020), Corporate citizenship is concerned about, 'the extent to which they [businesses] meet legal, ethical, and economic responsibilities'.

Jill Huntley (MD, Global Corporate Citizenship Accenture), states that at one level it is about 'how a company runs itself—its commitment to building trust by doing business ethically', and at another level, it is about the company's contribution to 'people, the economy and our planet'.

(Williams, n.d.)

In this framework, a company takes responsibility for its internal functioning and holds itself up to account for ethical behaviour, while at the same time taking responsibility for the impact it has on the neighbouring communities as well as on the larger society—from financial impacts to social and environmental ones.

Responsible Capitalism

A term related to Responsible Business, it implies a new kind of capitalism based on values that are broader than short-term profits. It is about developing a philosophy in which the company's success is not judged by short-term profits, but rather over the long term by benchmarks (including sustainability, equity and ethical behaviour) as well as financial parameters. In this framework, environmental and social needs—the needs of the wider society as well as those of the communities neighbouring a business—are taken into consideration and integrated into business decision making not as an afterthought but as a fundamental part of a corporation's objectives, plans, and processes. At its core, it is about business leaders bringing principles of ethics and social responsibility to bear on the way a business is operated, and optimizing social and environmental commitments through business processes and innovations.

Box 2.3: Enlightened Self-interest

Simply put, this is the belief that an individual, group, or business will 'do well by doing good'. It operates on the logic that managers are responsible to shareholders, and shareholders want the company to give them maximum return on their investment. Those who advocate for enlightened self-interest posit that the value of companies will increase if they are able to identify and be responsive to societal needs.

They believe that enlightened self-interest will work in various ways to help raise company value. For instance, it could increase market share by attracting customers who are sensitive to social and environmental issues; it could help in attracting good talent as young people now want to work for companies perceived to be responsible; it could help the business in gaining acceptance from the community; and it could help to secure future supplies of natural resources and raw material by working for their conservation.

Based on 'Examples of Enlightened Self-interest in Business', in *Chron* (2021)

Creating Shared Value

Management gurus Michael Porter and Mark Kramer (2011) define shared value as 'policies and operating practices that enhance the competitiveness of a company while simultaneously advancing the economic and social conditions in the communities in which it operates. Shared value creation focuses on identifying and expanding the connections between societal and economic progress.'

Creating shared value or CSV is sometimes referred to as a way of redefining capitalism. It takes the stand that well-being of a business is inextricably tied to the well-being of the communities around it, and that for a business to prosper it has to support the prosperity of its communities. It accepts that there may be a trade-off between short-term profits by taking into account social and environment goals, but sees a positive trade-off in terms of higher competitive advantage through this process of building a social value proposition into the core of the business strategy. As a management strategy, CSV looks to create measurable value for business by identifying and addressing social problems that overlap with business operations.

Shared Value Initiative Hong Kong (n.d.) notes that CSV can be created in the following ways:

1. By 'reconceiving markets and products': This entails defining markets in terms of social challenges or needs which are as yet unmet. This, in turn, includes redesigning products and services and their delivery to better meet societal needs, identifying unmet needs, or providing market solutions for social problems.
2. By 'redefining productivity of value chains': Here the idea is that a company can enhance its productivity through working on environmental and social constraints along its value chains; working on the efficiency of value chains; and by including more local businesses into these value chains, thereby increasing local livelihoods.
3. By 'enabling local cluster development': This is about strengthening the competitiveness of local suppliers and institutions, and thereby strengthening links of business success and community success.

Shared value does not advocate redistribution of the value created by profits, by route of donations, philanthropy, or CSR. Rather proponents say that CSV means basing the whole business on creation of value for both business and society, rather than seeing CSR as one of the activities of a business.

The idea is not for businesses to be 'good corporate citizens' through CSR, but rather to become 'better capitalists' or 'responsible capitalists' (ibid.). Proponents of CSV stress that it is fundamentally different in conception from CSR.

Sustainability and Sustainable Development Goals

The CSR gurus often cite 'sustainability' as the goal of CSR initiatives, or suggest that CSR programme outcomes be mapped to the Sustainable Development Goals (SDGs). So it is worth it to pause and get a little background on these terms.

The term 'Sustainable Development' started being discussed in the mid-1980s. A commission was set up by the then-UN Secretary General Javier Pérez de Cuéllar in 1983, headed by former prime minister of Norway, Gro Harlem Brundtland. The mandate given to the commission was to consider how the needs of environmental conservation could be balanced with development, leading to a long-term improvement in the quality of life for all. The commission, which commonly came to be referred to as the Brundtland Commission, explored reasons for degradation of the environment, attempted to lay down the interconnections between social equity, economic growth and environmental issues, and followed this up with policy suggestions for approaches that saw the three areas in an integrated and holistic fashion.

The Brundtland Commission report, also called *Our Common Future*, was released in 1987 by the World Commission on Environment and Development and defined Sustainable Development as 'development that meets the needs of the present without compromising the ability of future generations to meet their own needs'. Following this report, the concept of sustainable development became universally accepted, and today it is the common goal shared by all nations.

'Sustainability' refers to long-term viability. It is usually understood as 'ensuring the balance between economic growth, environmental care and social welfare'.

Sustainability is the goal—a future in which environmental, societal, and economic considerations are balanced in our quest for an improved quality of life. Sustainable development may be thought of as the path or the ways and means to achieve 'sustainability'. Corporate social responsibility too aims at contributing to a sustainable world, to economic and social development without environmental degradation. Hence, sustainable development and CSR are in sync.

Box 2.4: Circular Economy

A Circular Economy is proposed as an alternative paradigm to a Linear Economy which, as summed up by some thinkers, operates with a 'take-make-dispose' approach.

The Ellen McArthur Foundation (n.d) explains that the objective of a Circular Economy is to minimize resource input as well as wastes and emissions, while at the same time trying to regenerate natural resources. Focusing on making a business and the overall economy more environmentally sustainable, a Circular Economy is based on three principles:

- Design out waste and pollution
- Keep products and materials in use
- Regenerate natural systems

Based on: https://www.ellenmacarthurfoundation.org/circular-economy/concept

What are Sustainable Development Goals (SDGs)?

What is measured is what gets done. In order to measure the world's progress on the path of sustainable development, the international community has set itself SDGs, articulated by the United Nations Development Programme (UNDP) (www.undp.org).

Also known as the Global Goals, the SDGs were adopted by all United Nations member states in 2015 as a universal call to action to end poverty, protect the planet, and ensure that all people enjoy peace and prosperity by 2030. The SDGs are universally accepted as the development goals for the world, and India, like other countries, is obligated to work towards them.

The seventeen SDGs to be achieved by 2030 (ibid.) are:

1. End poverty in all its forms everywhere.
2. End hunger, achieve food security and improved nutrition, and promote sustainable agriculture.
3. Ensure healthy lives and promote well-being for all at all ages.
4. Ensure inclusive and equitable quality education and promote lifelong learning opportunities for all.
5. Achieve gender equality and empower all women and girls.
6. Ensure availability and sustainable management of water and sanitation for all.
7. Ensure access to affordable, reliable, sustainable, and modern energy for all.
8. Promote sustained, inclusive, and sustainable economic growth, full and productive employment, and decent work for all.
9. Build resilient infrastructure, promote inclusive and sustainable industrialization, and foster innovation.

10. Reduce inequality within and among countries.
11. Make cities and human settlements inclusive, safe, resilient, and sustainable.
12. Ensure sustainable consumption and production patterns.
13. Take urgent action to combat climate change and its impacts.
14. Conserve and sustainably use the oceans, seas, and marine resources for sustainable development.
15. Protect, restore, and promote sustainable use of terrestrial ecosystems, sustainably manage forests, combat desertification, halt and reverse land degradation, and halt loss of biodiversity.
16. Promote peaceful and inclusive societies for sustainable development, provide access to justice for all, and build effective, accountable, and inclusive institutions at all levels.
17. Strengthen the means of implementation and revitalize the global partnership for sustainable development.

The SDGs provide a very comprehensive framework to reach the ultimate objectives of Sustainability and Sustainable Development, and to monitor our progress towards these. Going through the SDGs, it is obvious that the goals are interrelated—initiatives in any one area will impact outcomes in another. For instance, ensuring inclusive and equitable quality education (Goal 4) will definitely help to achieve gender equality (Goal 5); or ensuring sanitation for all (Goal 6), will contribute to healthy lives for all (Goal 3).

To encourage the integration of SDG goals into core business goals and practices, UNDP has developed 'SDG Impact Standards' which are 'designed to transform how enterprises and investors think about value creation, and integrate impact management and contributing positively to the SDGs in their strategy, management approach, disclosure and governance practices' (sdgimpact.undp.org).

As we will see in subsequent sections, in India, Schedule VII of the Companies Act, 2013, lays down the thrust areas within which CSR initiatives can be taken up. Almost all of these can be mapped on to the SDGs, directly or indirectly. For instance, the very first thrust area mentioned in Schedule VII, namely, 'Eradicating hunger, poverty and malnutrition, promoting health care including preventive health care and sanitation', relates to SDGs 1, 2, 3, and 6. Similarly, actions under Schedule VII towards 'ensuring environmental sustainability, ecological balance, protection of flora and fauna, animal welfare, agroforestry, conservation of natural resources and maintaining quality of soil, air and water' will contribute to SDGs 7, 13, 14, 12, and 15.

(It may be noted that Schedule VII also includes some points such as preservation of cultural heritage, which are not part of the SDGs. It also has specific items which are relevant to the Indian context, such as taking actions to benefit war veterans, or contribution to various government funds.)

Though most CSR activities are linked to the SDGs, companies do not always see it in this framework, and CSR objectives and outcomes are therefore not articulated in SDG terms. It would be a useful exercise to map CSR programmes across SDGs, so that it becomes explicit as to which SDGs a company's activities are contributing towards. At the same time, it is necessary to map what SDGs the business itself is affecting, either positively or negatively, and to take relevant actions. This helps to link the local actions of the company to universal global goals, and also provides a way to link the impacts of the business with its CSR.

Human Development Index

The UNDP's work since the 1990s to 'shift the focus of development economics from national income accounting to people-centered policies', resulted in the development of the Human Development Index (HDI; www.undp.org). The HDI reiterates that ultimately, development is about the development of people and their capabilities; it is not just economic growth and GDP that tell us about the development of a country. The HDI is a consolidated measure of average achievement in key dimensions of human development that are articulated as:

- A long and healthy life (for which the best indicator is life expectancy at birth);
- Being knowledgeable (measured by expected years of schooling and mean years of schooling); and
- Having a decent standard of living (indicated by the Gross National Income).

In 2021, India's HDI ranking was 131 out of a total of 189 countries. Clearly, we have a very long way to go! Those CSR programmes that focus on issues such as education, health, skilling, livelihoods, etc., have the potential to contribute to improving HDI at local level.

Other International Standards and Non-Financial Reporting Protocols

There are several international reporting protocols, standards, and measures which are relevant to CSR. In fact, there are so many that it would be quite confusing to try to discuss all of them. However, it is definitely useful to be introduced to some major ones.

In this context it is important to understand the term 'Non-Financial Reporting' (NFR), as most of the systems discussed below fall under this category. Non-Financial Reporting is 'the practice of measuring, disclosing and being accountable to internal and external stakeholders for organizational performance towards the goal of sustainable and inclusive development'. In India, the recently introduced Business Responsibility and Sustainability Reporting protocol is the officially mandated NFR format for the top 1,000 largest businesses, and is also recommended to be undertaken voluntarily by others. Internationally, there are several others. Major NFR Protocols include the following:

The United Nations Global Compact (UNGC)

The UNGC is a set of principles that an organization—no matter whether it is a corporate or an NGO, or what the business is, or where it is operating—can voluntarily sign on to. It lays down the basic principles on which the organization will run the business. The underlying philosophy is that corporate sustainability can come about when the value system of a company is right, and when business is conducted based on principles. It means running the business so that at the very least the basic responsibilities vis-à-vis human rights, labour relations, environment, and anti-corruption are met. It implies that responsible organizations, irrespective of where they operate, should live by a consistent set of values and principles. Having signed on, the organization has to submit an annual Communication on Progress.

The UNGC principles help to avoid, for instance, the kind of problem one often reads about, of multinational companies having different standards of conduct in their home countries as compared to countries where their factories may be located. The UNGC also recognizes that there is no trade-off;

in other words, doing well in one area does not compensate for harm in another. By integrating the UNGC principles into vision, strategies, policies, and systems, and by striving towards an environment of integrity, companies can fulfil their responsibilities to people and planet, and also lay the foundation for long-term success.

The ten principles of the UNGC (www.unglobalcompact.org) are covered under the following four heads:

1. Human Rights

   Principle 1: Businesses should support and respect the protection of internationally proclaimed human rights; and
   Principle 2: make sure that they are not complicit in human rights abuses.

2. Labour Standards

   Principle 3: Businesses should uphold the freedom of association and effective recognition of the right to collective bargaining;
   Principle 4: the elimination of all forms of forced and compulsory labour;
   Principle 5: the effective abolition of child labour; and
   Principle 6: the elimination of discrimination in employment and occupation.

3. Environment

   Principle 7: Businesses should support a precautionary approach to environmental challenges;

Principle 8: undertake initiatives to promote environmental responsibility; and

Principle 9: encourage the development and diffusion of environmentally friendly technologies.

4. Anti-Corruption

Principle 10: Businesses should work against corruption in all its forms, including extortion and bribery.

As of 2022, 389 organizations from India, ranging from small and medium industries to large multinationals to NGOs and various foundations, were signatories to the UNGC.

Sustainability Reporting and Global Reporting Initiative

A 'sustainability report' is an instrument through which a company reports its environmental and social impacts to its stakeholders. The report also communicates the organization's values and governance model, and attempts to show how its strategy is consistent with its commitment to a sustainable global economy.

The Global Reporting Initiative (GRI; www.globalreporting.org) format is one of the most widely used for sustainability reporting and includes disclosures in the economic, environmental, and social categories. Thus reporting under GRI attempts to present a complete picture of both governance practices as well as the environmental and social impacts of a business. In fact, it is concerned not just about the corporate entity in view, but looks at the whole value chain—for instance, the environmental or labour practices of suppliers.

Given its very wide scope, GRI asks about everything—from details about a company's donations to political parties, to governance structures (including decision-making processes regarding environmental and social dimensions), to procurement processes, anti-corruption measures, details of stakeholder involvement, and so on.

Listing some of the items in the GRI framework gives us an idea of its holistic approach. The environmental category includes reporting usage of material, energy and water; and impacts on biodiversity, emissions, effluents, and waste. The social category includes reporting on labour practices and decent work, human rights, indigenous communities and local communities, among other areas.

Going through the reporting process under GRI is an opportunity for a corporate to introspect on all aspects of governance and social responsibility and evaluate itself on these, and hence creates room for improvement.

Environmental, Social and Governance (ESG) Rating

Under this international system which is essentially a risk-management tool, ESG performance of a corporate is assessed on three criteria: environmental, social, and governance. A set of indicators is defined for each criterion, which evaluates the company's performance within that. Under the environment criterion, the factors considered include climate change, natural resources, pollution and waste, and environmental opportunities. In the social bucket, the focus is on human capital, product liability, stakeholder opposition, and social opportunities; and in the governance section, corporate governance and corporate behaviour are taken into account. Based on performance, companies are rated as Laggards, Average, or Leaders. It is a sector rating so that companies in similar contexts are compared. The UN too has brought out a set of principles to guide investment on ESG lines, termed UN Principles for Responsible Investment.

Rating is usually done on the basis of annual filings and information from other sources. In addition, ongoing monitoring of companies is done with regard to any controversial issue arising which pertains to ESG. An issue such as a corporate's involvement or connection with negative incidents and controversies can potentially result in higher risk to investors. Such negative events are categorized across the E, S and G pillars and are given scores depending on the reputational risk to the company and potential impact on stakeholders. Information for this may be drawn from media, NGOs and other stakeholders.

Globally, already about 30 per cent of investments take into account some type of ESG screening, and ESG investments are forecast to triple in the coming decade. This is also rapidly gaining importance in India. India has the NIFTY100 ESG Index which is designed to reflect the performance of companies within the NIFTY 100 index, based on ESG scores (www.nseindia.com). There are several ESG Funds today that offer investment opportunities and corporates need to be conscious of the fact that ESG will become increasingly critical if they want to retain their investments.

Other International Reporting Protocols

Integrated reporting

Not commonly undertaken by Indian companies, these reports are based on a holistic perspective of an organization's value creation over time. As per the International Integrated Reporting Council, an integrated report communicates how an organization's strategy, governance, and performance lead to the creation of value in the short, medium, and long terms.

Sustainability and Accountability Standards Board (SASB)

The SASB develops industry-specific standards for reporting on ESG issues. These standards currently span across seventy-seven industries. The purpose is to help companies and investors to communicate meaningfully on 'financially material, decision-useful information' (www.sasb.org).

Box 2.5: Materiality

The challenge with regard to CSR and sustainability reporting is often that it may not focus on what is relevant, critical, and important in a particular situation. 'Materiality' is therefore an important consideration.

Materiality means ensuring that reporting:

- reflects 'the organization's significant economic, environmental, and social impacts'; and
- covers 'matters that can substantively influence the assessments and decisions of stakeholders'.

Based on: https://www.povertyactionlab.org/sites/default/files/

Dow Jones Sustainability Index

This index comprises global sustainability leaders as identified by S&P through Corporate Sustainability Assessment (CSA). It represents the top 10 per cent of the largest 2,500 companies in the S&P Global Broad Market Index (BMI) based on long-term economic, environmental, and social criteria. It 'comprises global sustainability leaders, as identified by S&P Global through the Corporate Sustainability Assessment' (www.spglobal.com). The assessment is based on an analysis of corporate economic, environmental, and social performance and covers issues including corporate governance, risk management, branding, climate change mitigation, supply chain standards, and labour practices. The assessment is done on overall criteria as well as industry-specific ones.

Some Related Certifications and Standards

ISO 26000

This is an ISO standard related to CSR and is discussed in further detail later in the book.

B Corps

Companies certified under B Corps 'meet the highest standards of verified social and environmental performance, public transparency, and legal accountability to balance profit and purpose' (www.bcorporation.net).

The certification takes into account everything from supply chains and input materials to charitable giving and employee benefits. It rests on the following principles (ibid.):

- Each leader and business must be the change they seek in the world.
- All businesses ought to be conducted as if people and place mattered.
- Through their products, practices, and profits, businesses should aspire to do no harm and benefit all.
- To do so requires that they act with the understanding that each is dependent upon another and thus responsible for each other and future generations.

International Financial Corporation (IFC) Performance Standards

The IFC Performance Standards are applicable for those entities who have borrowed from financial institutions funded by IFC (www.ifc.org). There are eight IFC Performance Standards which IFC expects companies to meet. These standards require companies to go beyond minimum compliance with the local laws, and reflect and embody the concept of sustainable development.

The standards relate to (ibid.)

- Assessment and management of environmental and social risks and impacts;
- Labour and working conditions;
- Resource efficiency and pollution prevention;
- Community health, safety, and security;
- Land acquisition and involuntary resettlement;
- Biodiversity conservation and sustainable management of living natural resources;
- Indigenous peoples; and
- Cultural heritage.

FTSE4Good

FTSE4Good Index Series is a measure of the performance of companies in meeting globally recognized corporate responsibility standards, and aims to help investors to identify ethical and responsible companies (see www.ftserussell.com). It looks at a company's support to human rights, its relationships with various stakeholders, its progress to become environmentally sustainable, ensuring good labour standards not only for their own company but for companies that supply them as well, and fighting bribery and corruption. Currently, this is not applicable to India and other emerging markets.

Some Emerging Concepts

Those working in CSR will come across new concepts and terms every day. Some of these are indeed new ideas. Others are concepts which are becoming popular in India of late, or are being reframed in our context. Here is a round-up of some of them.

Social Entrepreneurship

As per the Yunus Centre set up by Nobel Laureate Muhammad Yunus, the pioneer of social entrepreneurship:

> A social business is a non-dividend business whose aim is to solve a social problem through business methods. It is different from both a traditional personal profit-making business and a not-for-profit organization.
>
> All profits from operation of the business must go toward achieving one or more social objectives in addition to covering costs of the company. No personal

> gain is desired by its investors. A social business can address problems such as providing healthcare, housing, and financial services for the poor, nutrition for malnourished children, providing safe drinking water, introducing renewable energy and much more in a business way (https://muhammadyunus.org/).

Simply put, social entrepreneurship is doing business for a social cause. It is a business that combines commercial approaches and social issues in a way that improves the lives of people. Success is not measured in terms of profit alone; it is mainly measured in terms of how the business has improved the world. Hence, social enterprises are businesses with a social purpose, set up to achieve positive change in the world around. They aim to achieve large-scale change, and use innovative approaches to bring this about.

For instance, putting up pay-and-use toilets in cities where there are otherwise no public conveniences, as Sulabh India has so successfully done, is a social enterprise. Not only is it a business in the sense that it generates income and makes some surplus, but it also meets a real need while it helps to keep our cities and towns cleaner and more hygienic, and provides sanitation workers with better and more dignified working conditions.

Setting up Water ATMs in villages with no drinking-water supply, through which households can buy water for a very reasonable rate, is another example of a social enterprise. Setting up a mechanism for women to make and market craft products and hence improve their incomes could be a social enterprise.

Social entrepreneurship is not new to India—Amul and Fabindia are oft-quoted examples of highly successful social enterprises (see Box 2.6).

Box 2.6: AMUL—Collective Ownership for Common Good

Today, India is the world's largest producer of milk. Over 160 lakh milk producers across the country contribute milk to over 1.8 lakh dairy cooperatives, and this is brought to consumers by 28 state marketing federations.

The story started in Kheda district of Gujarat in pre-Independence days, when farmers came together under the leadership of people like Sardar Vallabhbhai Patel, Morarji Desai, and Tribhuvandas Patel to organize themselves against exploitation by middlemen. They formed a cooperative society in 1946, starting with just two village dairy cooperatives producing 247 litres of milk. Soon Dr Verghese Kurien joined and took the movement from strength to strength. The movement ensured that milk producers and consumers were linked directly, through their own organizations, thus avoiding intermediaries. Elected representatives managed village societies and district unions, while professionals were employed to run the operations. The whole structure was sensitive and responsive to farmer needs.

This has not only made India such a large milk producer, but has added wealth to each of the 160 lakh milk-producing families.

A social enterprise indeed!

Based on https://www.amul.com/

The Companies Act, 2013, excludes the term 'social business' in the list of permissible CSR activities on which corporates could spend their CSR funds. There may however be ways to support some of these initiatives through CSR—for instance, supporting an NGO to construct a community toilet through CSR funds is allowable. After the construction, the NGO may choose to run it on a pay-and-use basis, with a commitment to charge a fee affordable by the community and to use the generated funds to only maintain and improve the facility. This does not violate the spirit of CSR provisions. Similarly, collaborations and partnerships between social entrepreneurs, NGOs and corporates can be beneficial to the CSR space, and have the potential to bring in new models.

Impact Investing

The Global Impact Investing Network (GIIN) defines Impact Investing as 'investments made with the intention to generate positive, measurable social and environmental impact alongside a financial return' (thegiin.org). The level of social impact depends on the investor's goals, while financial returns in such ventures range from below-market to market rates. Philanthropy expects no returns on what it gives. But impact investors expect some financial returns along with measurable social and environmental impacts. Healthcare, education, clean energy, and agriculture are some of the sectors where impact investing funds are often focused.

Impact investing is an emerging paradigm which aims to blur the chasm between traditional understanding of business as exclusively focused on making a profit, and public policy and non-profit operations which are seen as means to achieving social progress. Impact funding is seen as investment into a new approach to social service delivery.

Nowadays, private and family foundations and endowments, development banks, charitable organizations and individuals are showing increasing interest in impact investing.

To put it in the context of the CSR discussion, social enterprises and impact investing achieve the same ends as community development projects under CSR do, but through market-based approaches. Social entrepreneurship and impact investing want to make a difference like CSR, philanthropy, and charity; they aim to make the world a better place. But social entrepreneurship and impact investing are different in that they want to solve social problems through a market or business approach.

Green Banking

According to the Organization for Economic Cooperation and Development (OECD), a Green Bank is 'a public, quasi-public or non-profit entity established specifically to facilitate private investment into domestic low-carbon, climate-resilient infrastructure' (www.oecd.org). Basically, a Green Bank is a financial institution that uses innovative financing methods and market development, in order to give a fillip to deployment of clean energy technologies. Such an entity's efforts are towards accelerating the movement towards a low-carbon economy.

Ethical Investing

This is an investing process that takes into account the investor's personal values (whether social, moral, religious, political, or environmental) prior to making the investment decisions. For instance, there may be an institution or individual averse to any of their investments going into any company which even remotely has anything to do with alcohol. Ethical investing helps them make these choices. Ethical investing may be done through considering 'positive impact', i.e., choosing industries, sectors, and companies with values similar to those of the investor; or through 'negative impacting', i.e., avoiding industries, sectors, and companies with values not in consonance with the investor's values (corporatefinanceinstitute.com). For instance, ESG funds are an example of ethical investing in that they invest only in companies which are doing well on environmental, social, and governance fronts.

Social Stock Exchange

The setting up of a Social Stock Exchange (SSE) is under active discussion in India. An SSE would allow listing of non-profits and NGOs on stock exchanges. This provides an alternative route for fund-raising, rather than just depending on donations, grants, and project funds. As per preliminary discussions, such an entity may be listed on the Bombay Stock Exchange (BSE) or the National Stock Exchange (NSE), and would be able to raise money through bonds, social venture funds, and mutual funds. At the same time, significant emphasis is being laid on incorporating 'a set of procedures by which social impact will be measured and reported' (www.sebi.gov.in).

3

A Vexed Question: Does CSR Really Help Business?

The answer to this question, as also to many other questions in this book, is not straightforward. If one interprets 'help' as strengthening the bottom line, research has yet to return an unqualified 'YES' as the answer. Many studies have indeed proved a positive link between CSR and corporate financial performance (CFP), but a few have thrown up inconclusive results. There are even a few that indicate negative correlation! It is difficult to conclusively prove direct correlation and causality between increased CSR and improved financial performance, especially in the short run.

But that is just the point! CSR is not meant to be about the bottom line of profit. It is meant to be about the Triple Bottom Line of profit, people, and planet, and about better governance through integrating concerns of all stakeholders into business decision making. In other words, CSR can lead to a more sustainable business, and hence 'help' the business, but not necessarily in a way that will be reflected in quarterly results and market values of the corporate stocks in the short run.

Here is a look at some of the indirect ways that CSR has been shown to help businesses.

Social Licence: Fundamental to Operations

A business or project may be said to have social licence when it has the ongoing approval of the local community and other stakeholders to carry on its business. A stakeholder may be defined as an individual, group, or institution with an interest in a business, and who is either affected by it or can affect it. Primary stakeholders are those who have a direct relationship with the business and include investors, staff, customers, communities and suppliers. Secondary stakeholders are those not directly connected with the business—such as competitors, media, advocacy groups, and government organizations at local, state, or national levels—but can have some level of influence over its workings.

Social licence (ongoing approval for the business to operate) stems from the opinions and perceptions of both groups of stakeholders. For instance, even after formal clearances, if a community feels that a project is causing them harm—maybe through pollution, or withdrawal of too much groundwater, or not contributing to the local economy by providing jobs to local youth—it witholds approval through various means (non-cooperation, litigations, strikes, obstructions to operations, etc.), thus not giving the project social licence. It can then become difficult for the project to continue or a business to operate.

Thus it becomes important for businesses to work with communities with a win-win vision, integrating their concerns into business decision making—in other words, operationalizing stakeholder focus of the business in the true sense. This may result in modifying business decisions, such as making a commitment to employ a certain percentage of local youth in the business, or committing to less water-intensive manufacturing processes so as not to deplete the water tables, and so on. Needless to say, CSR has a role in this too, through fostering such relationships and supplementing the business action with CSR programmes. For instance, if the business commits to employing local youth, the CSR programme can help to skill them. Or if the business is integrating water conservation in the manufacturing plant, the CSR programme can take up watershed programmes in the neighbouring areas.

Box 3.1: Nursing Care for the North-east.

National CSR Award for Contribution to National Priority Area: Women and Child Development

Indian Oil, which has a large presence in Assam, established the Assam Oil School of Nursing in 1986 as part of its CSR programme. It started with offering a three-year diploma in nursing, and in 2014, started a four-year course in BSc nursing. The initiative covers nine cities and forty-seven districts of Assam, and has an annual intake of sixty students. Close to 450 students have successfully completed their courses, and the Assam Oil School of Nursing has a 100 per cent placement record.

Not only does the School help to fill the gap of qualified nurses in the state, it also provides opportunities for underprivileged girls to attain professional qualifications and thus pursue good careers.

Based on https://iocl.com/aboutus/Awards-and-Recognitions.aspx

Enhancing Brand Image

A company known to be socially responsible naturally commands the trust and respect of all stakeholders and the public at large. This gives the company a good standing and can affect a number of factors positively—from perception of the bureaucracy about the business to its standing in the stock market. Such a brand image is built over time and through a series of experiences that the stakeholders have with the company. In India for instance, some groups like the Tatas and TVS command an image that compels trust.

Increasing Customer Loyalty

Customers, especially younger ones, are increasingly concerned about the way products and services they consume are produced. So if a company is known to be more environmentally responsible, it is likely to attract and retain customers. Similarly, if there are suspicions that a company even remotely or indirectly employs child labour, there may be a very adverse reaction among a large section of its clientele.

Box 3.2: The Nike Saga

Nike, the famous shoe company has been plagued for over two decades now by accusations of employing child labour, paying very low wages, and lately, of employing forced labour. The company has denied these accusations and also tried to explain them. To quote a report by Steve Boggan in *The Independent* (Boggan, 2001):

> Philip Knight, the company chairman, clearly stung by reports of children as young as 10 making shoes, clothing and footballs in Pakistan and Cambodia, attempted to convince Nike's critics that it had only ever employed children accidentally. 'Of all the issues facing Nike in workplace standards, child labor is the most vexing,' he said in the report. 'Our age standards are the highest in the world: 18 for footwear manufacturing, 16 for apparel and equipment, or local standards whenever they are higher. But in some countries (Bangladesh and Pakistan, for example) those standards are next to impossible to verify, when records of birth do not exist or can be easily forged.'

Whatever the explanations, there is no denying that these issues are extremely grave, and have been taken seriously by NGOs, human rights groups, as well as consumers.

Enhancing Employee Morale

Employees are attracted to join socially responsible companies; they also gain social respect by working in such companies. For employees already working in such a company, opportunities to engage with communities through CSR and employee-engagement programmes are not only a matter of pride but also of motivation. Such projects can help to reinforce the larger purpose and context of the business, and also give scope for employees to develop a different set of networks and competencies. Putting employees into situations where they have to engage with social and environmental challenges can also promote innovation, which may have positive business impacts. Hence CSR initiatives can have positive impacts on HR management and implications for attracting and retaining talent.

Box 3.3: Integrating the Differently Abled

National CSR Award to Minda Corporation for Contribution to National Priority Area: Support to Differently Abled

Saksham, an initiative of the Spark Minda Foundation of the Minda Corporation, has a holistic approach to working with the differently abled. This includes providing accessible and assistive technologies widely through camps and other interventions.

Critically, Saksham also provides on-the-job training for the differently abled, and the company maps out suitable jobs for different types of abilities within its operations, and employs Persons with Disabilities (PWD) as per the mapping. The workplace is made inclusive through modifying both structural and 'soft' aspects. PWDs are provided training in 5S and life skills, as well as evacuation procedures in case of emergencies.

Based on: https://sparkminda.com/csrminda/

Gaining Access to Capital

Banks and financial institutions are deeply concerned about the governance practices of a company as well as the risk. Thus CSR programmes, especially those which are well integrated with the business, are a demonstration that these factors are being given their due importance. Sometimes financial institutions, e.g, IFC, have laid-down standards with regard to social and environmental concerns, and appreciate the proactive steps taken by corporates in demonstrating responsibility in this direction. Today, ESG ratings are gaining importance too. Hence, well-designed and effectively implemented CSR can help a corporate in accessing capital.

Helping in Cost Savings and Business Expansion

If CSR is viewed not merely as a spend on community programmes, but as a way of thinking about how business is conducted, then the cost-savings angle comes out clearly. For instance, take the simple example of a manufacturing unit. If it decides to reduce its environmental footprint, it will take all measures to reduce its energy consumption, water use, paper use, waste, etc. All these obviously lead to better housekeeping and cost savings. The same can be extended to facilities like airports or service units like hotels, etc. For instance, the move to give hotel guests the option of not having their towels changed every day is not only environmentally friendly, but a huge cost saving for the business too! In fact Porter and Kramer (2006) feel that many corporates are missing out on the opportunities that CSR can offer for business, by not understanding its potential. They say:

> If corporations were to analyze their opportunities for social responsibility using the same frameworks that guide their core business choices, they would discover ... that CSR can be much more than a cost, a constraint, or a charitable deed—it can be a potent source of innovation and competitive advantage (ibid.).

Promoting Long-term Thinking

Strategic CSR, which is basically about taking into account the interests of all stakeholders, shifts the focus within a business towards long-term thinking. For instance, if a company is interested only in quarterly profits, the decisions it takes would be different from what they would be if it were concerned about sustainability and long-term health. For instance, a company may decide to switch to solar power in the interests of long-term sustainability—both environmental and financial—even if it costs more in money terms in the present.

So, apart from benefit to communities, CSR has very real benefits for the corporate itself. The moral imperative is probably that CSR is not done *for* these reasons, but that these be viewed as collateral benefits resulting from a mindset which wants a win-win for the corporate, the community, and the environment.

A few concepts, related to this thinking are elaborated upon below in the context of CSR and returns to business.

Making CSR Strategic

As we briefly saw, many (though not all) studies have pointed to some positive correlation between CSR and CFP. Through examining the cases studied, scholars have been able to identify some reasons for the positive link of CSR leading to CFP. The most significant ones operate through four mechanisms.

Enhancing corporate reputation

It has been demonstrated that strong positive messaging about a firm's CSR activities and its contribution to society and the community lead to the perception that the firm is a better partner to work with, a better employer, more trustworthy, etc., and these factors in turn are directly linked to better financial performance.

Increasing stakeholder reciprocation

When companies take actions to improve their relationship with a particular stakeholder, the stakeholder reciprocates, and hence this leads to better financial performance. For instance, if a company invests in the local community through improving local infrastructure, health and education facilities, and livelihood opportunities, the community is more likely to support the smooth running of the business.

Mitigating business risk

Risk mitigation happens in two ways. Sometimes, CSR activities are designed so as to reduce negative impacts on stakeholders, e.g., pollution prevention over and above legal requirements, which reduce the community's exposure to harm. This also leads to a mitigation of risk to the firm. Risk may also indirectly be reduced by CSR. For instance, a company seriously focused on CSR has more communication with its stakeholders and hence enjoys greater goodwill with them. In turn, its stakeholders are then more willing to share information with the company, which helps to increase the company's awareness of community needs and become more responsive, leading to increased goodwill. And if there are any changes or threats in the environment, the company gets to know about these and is able to prepare for any adverse eventualities.

Strengthening innovation capacity

Again, by being in closer communication with various sections of internal and external stakeholders, companies that are more CSR-oriented are able to become aware of opportunities more quickly and act upon them in a more timely manner. Furthermore, CSR can improve the firm's innovativeness because adoption of CSR activities may lead to development of new products and services. For instance, it may lead to low-cost solutions for drinking water problems, pollution prevention or green energy challenges, which could lead to cost savings for the company, or may even become another business arm.

These four mechanisms are seen as ways to make CSR strategic. In other words, if the CSR plan consciously brings into play one or more of these, it becomes strategic. Of course, there is always the criticism that such CSR may be cynically undertaken with the sole view of reaping these benefits (as opposed to being done for the primary reason of being responsible). It may be true that some firms may practise it from these angles. That being said, while CSR needs to be undertaken for the right reasons, it must also bring good to the company. The wisdom lies in not letting the tail wag the dog.

One concept of CSR activities which adds strategic advantage to a firm as given by Vishwanathan et al. (2020) is that of all the activities carried out by a firm, many contribute to its corporate financial performance (CFP). A smaller number contribute towards social good. There is a small area of overlap between CSR and CFP-enhancing activities—these are the ones that could be termed as Strategic CSR.

Strategic CSR

William Werther and David Chandler (2011) approach strategic CSR in a more fundamental manner. Chandler (2019) notes:

> [...] strategic CSR is related to, but is fundamentally different from, concepts such as sustainability and business ethics. While sustainability focuses on resource utilization and ecological preservation, and business ethics seeks to construct normative prescriptions of right and wrong, strategic CSR is grounded in the day-to-day operations of the firm. As such, strategic CSR is central to the firm's value-creating activities.

He opines that in defining 'CSR as core to business operations and value creation (as opposed to peripheral practices that can be marginalized within the firm), these defining principles become applicable across the range of operational functions. In the process, they redefine how businesses approach each of these functions in practice' (ibid.).

Risk Mitigation and CSR

Every organization has to face several risk factors. And every organization has to protect itself against risk. While it may seem cynical to view CSR as a risk-management strategy, there is no doubt that this is consciously or subconsciously in the minds of managements as they develop their approach to CSR and sustainability—environmental, social, financial, and organizational. The ESG approaches are about managing social, environmental, and governance concerns from a risk perspective.

Each company faces its own set of risks depending on its sector, geography, and its unique characteristics. From the point of view of developing a material and relevant CSR strategy, risks may be broadly categorized as below:

Environmental risk

This covers threats to the environment brought about on one hand by a company's emissions, effluents, or wastes, and on the other by activities that lead to depletion of natural resources.

Reputation risk

Any action of the corporate that reduces the trust of members, employees, community, or the general public regarding its integrity or capability is a reputation risk. For instance, a leak in a chemical plant or factory, even when it does not lead to any negative consequence, could be a reputation risk. Today's consumers are extremely socially and environmentally conscious, and such an incident may even destroy a company.

While proper and adequate pollution control and risk management systems have to be in place, a CSR programme that keeps the community informed about the chemicals used in the factory, undertakes disaster management training, and equips local healthcare institutions for taking care of any accidents, would be elements of a strategy to mitigate risk to reputation. If CSR programmes can help to not just mitigate risk but actually build reputation in this manner, it is a bonus. Many young consumers would like to buy goods and services if they know the company is proactive in supporting environmental or social causes.

Social risks

These are risks associated with the workplace (e.g., labour and working conditions, occupational health, etc.), as well as those impacting local communities (e.g., community health and safety, issues related to land acquisition and loss of livelihoods, rehabilitation and resettlement, indigenous people, threats to cultural heritage, etc.), arising out of the operations of a company.

Operational risk

This is the risk of loss or harm resulting from internal processes or systems that are not strong or which fail, and risk from people or events in the external environment. For instance, stoppage of work due to a strike or dharna outside a manufacturing unit by youth demanding jobs in the manufacturing unit. A relevant CSR programme could redress this by supporting skilling and placement of youth in jobs and also supporting micro enterprises to help youth become self-employed.

Credit risk

This pertains to the risk of losses arising because a borrower fails to repay loans or to pay for services. Banks, and non-banking finance companies (NBFCs), etc., can be especially vulnerable to this. Hence, it would be relevant if their CSR programmes were focused on improving the overall economic health of the communities they work in—maybe through agriculture support programmes, women self-help group (SHG) programmes, etc.—so that borrowers and clients are strengthened to pay on time.

Governance risks

This pertains to the risk arising from the mismanagement of a company's internal affairs (e.g., lack of proper accounting systems and transparency, conflict of interests, etc.), and the adverse impacts of this on its relationships with the company's stakeholders.

Environment, social, and governance ratings are essentially focused on risk, and are a way in which a company is rated by the market based on its perception of the company's ESG risks. This form of rating is rapidly becoming prevalent across the world.

As we have seen in the Nike example (see Box 3.2) a supplier's factory in a developing country which employs child labour or has inadequate or unsafe working conditions or practices is a huge risk (apart of course from being morally untenable!). There may also be significant risk in their supply chain management and this is one area they need to focus on. Hence, often CSR activities of many enlightened multinationals tend to focus on occupational health and safety above and beyond what the local law requires them to do. In many cases, apart from ensuring that their supplier facilities do not pollute, they go further and have environmental conservation or restoration programmes.

Risk management as a collateral benefit of a well-designed CSR programme makes good strategic sense. The problem is only when a corporate uses CSR primarily as a risk-management tool. The business world needs to move towards putting social and environmental considerations on par with financial considerations, at the heart of decision making. With regard to the vexed question of whether CSR in the traditionally understood sense helps business, Rangan, Chase and Karim (2015) provide useful insights to put things into perspective: 'If ... CSR activities mitigate risks, enhance reputation, and contribute to business results, that is all to the good. But for many CSR programs, those outcomes should be a spillover, not their reason for being.'

4

CSR in India: A Background

The CSR Tradition in India

The belief that social responsibility goes beyond the purview of the government, and that every individual and institution has a part to play in this, has been inherent to Indian thinking through the ages. For instance, the Rig Veda has a chapter devoted to charity, dharma, karma, reverence for life, and recognition of the interconnectedness of life. Every religion advocates giving, and even today these concepts probably influence our understanding of charity, of philanthropy, and to some extent, CSR. The shape of giving, however, changes with time.

Though India has such a long history of philanthropy and the contribution of businesses to development, scholars like Sundar (2000), lament that there is very little knowledge or appreciation in India of the history, scope, and nature of business contribution to development, or the potential this has to transform society. She points out that there is dearth of historical work on Indian philanthropy (ibid.).

However, some trends are clear. The late nineteenth and early twentieth centuries were when Indian businesses grew significantly and newer ways of giving became dominant, essentially led by businesses and very wealthy individuals who had made their money from business. In fact some scholars say that in the early nineteenth century, apart from the Western world, the CSR concept was significantly developed only in Japan and India. 'Giving' in this phase was more secular and institutionally focused than in earlier times. While the tradition of supporting causes such as education and healthcare continued from the days of pure charity, the way it was now operationalized was different. There was a greater thrust on institutionalization and a focus on working through intermediary institutions (ibid.).

The period between the two World Wars was a time of fast-paced change. Indian businesses grew hugely, and the movement for independence gathered momentum. This saw a different type of social responsibility. Businesses were highly influenced by Gandhian thought and supported the nation's efforts for industrial and social development. Their agendas were influenced by the political and social issues of the time. The freedom movement itself was a cause which attracted significant contributions from business houses (ibid.).

Box 4.1: Gandhi Ashram is Saved!

When Gandhiji first came to Ahmedabad, he set up his ashram at Kochrab. He invited a Dalit couple—Dudabhai and Danibehn—to come and live at the ashram. This led to considerable agitation among the ashram's neighbours as well as many funders, leading to a financial crisis which forced Gandhiji to think of shifting the ashram.

And then one day, in Gandhiji's words:

> A car drew up near our quarters and the horn was blown. The children came with the news. The sheth did not come in. I went out to see him. He placed in my hands currency notes to the value of Rs 13,000 and drove away. I had never expected this help, and what a novel way of rendering it! (Mehta, 2019)

This gift saved the Ashram. It is well known that the 'Sheth' was Ambalal Sarabhai, one of the foremost industrialists of the time. However, neither he nor Gandhiji ever admitted this!

After Independence, up until maybe 1980, the government's approach towards business was dominated by a focus on legal regulation. The trend was to support the public sector and CSR was also shaped by this thinking. In the 1960s and '70s, CSR appears to have been dominated by the welfare efforts of public sector undertakings through their townships and social initiatives.

After this came the phase when CSR was largely dominated by community development initiatives. Much of this was on charitable lines and guided by the perspectives of the founder families. In the last decades of the twentieth century, CSR in India inched towards a phase of a wider and more internationally aligned thinking on the Triple Bottom Line, sustainability, etc.

Some Significant Milestones

Indian visionaries have given significant thought to the role of business in society. Gandhi summed up his concept of the contribution of business to society in terms of trusteeship: 'moneyed men may earn their crores (honestly only, of course) but so as to dedicate them to the service of all' (Gandhi, 1942). In fact, it may be said that even at present, perspectives on social responsibility in the country are to some extent influenced by the Gandhian model of voluntary commitment to public welfare and the needs of society.

There were many business people and business houses that strongly influenced thinking on social responsibility in the early days, including the Tatas, Birlas and Bajajs. The strong views of the Tatas on the subject are well known. Jamsetji Tata significantly shaped the corporate culture towards 'service to the wider community and high ethical standards' (Jones, 2018), and this legacy continues to this day.

It was private philanthropy that led to the creation of institutions like the Indian Institute of Science (IISc) in Bengaluru and Tata Institute for Fundamental Research (TIFR), Mumbai. It is said that J.N. Tata mooted the idea of contributing to an institute like IISc as early as 1898, long before Carnegie's endowment to set up a technical school (today's Carnegie Mellon University).

Jamnalal Bajaj was another strong influence. His financial support to the freedom struggle, the family's active participation in the freedom movement, his view that business had the patriotic duty to free India from the British, and most importantly, his affirmation of Gandhiji's trusteeship model of capitalism and his insistence that it mattered how business made money were radical not just for those times.

Box 4.2: Jamnalal Bajaj—Exemplary Patriotism

Jamnalal Bajaj was considered Gandhiji's fifth son and adopted all his values—from ahimsa (non-violence) to his dedication to the poor, to his commitment to locally made goods, and his patriotic spirit. He fought for admission of Harijans into temples, and in the face of strong objections, opened up his own family temple in Wardha—the first temple in the country to do this.

Bajaj was an active member of the Congress party, and gave up the Rai Bahadur title conferred on him by the British government and joined the non-cooperation movement.

Importantly, Jamnalalji, in line with the trusteeship concept propounded by Gandhiji, felt that inherited wealth was a sacred trust to be used for the benefit of the people, and dedicated most of his wealth for the poor and underprivileged.

Based on: https://jamnalalbajajfoundation.org/jamnalal-bajaj/about

The Role of the Public Sector

Since Independence, the role of the public sector in national development has been extremely important in the Indian context. The setting up of public sector units (PSUs) was not only aimed towards industrial production in key sectors, but was also meant to ensure inclusive growth and achieve equity and justice for communities and society. These missions were integrated into the charters of these organizations, and their very creation and existence remain driven by societal objectives, going well beyond commercial ones. This is CSR in the deepest sense. For instance, the public sector explicitly aims to support balanced regional development, through location of units in backward areas where private capital may hesitate to go. The setting up of such units brings about development of infrastructure in these areas, as also employment opportunities.

Box 4.3: Vision Statements of some Central PSUs

Airports Authority of India: To be the foundation of an enduring Indian aviation network, providing high quality, safe and customer-oriented airport and air navigation services, thereby acting as a catalyst for economic growth in the areas we serve.

Coal India: To emerge as a global player in the primary energy sector committed to provide energy security to the country by attaining environmentally and socially sustainable growth through best practices from mine to market.

National Mineral Development Corporation: To emerge as a global environment-friendly mining organization and also as a quality steel producer with a positive thrust on social development.

Oil and Natural Gas Corporation: To be global leader in integrated energy business through sustainable growth, knowledge excellence, and exemplary governance practices.

In fact today, the mandates for government companies with regard to CSR are even more stringent than for private companies, and PSUs are among the biggest CSR spenders. For instance, in 2019–20, the CSR spend by 455 PSUs was Rs 5,270 crore, while that of 22,209 non-PSU companies was Rs 19,593 crore. As can be seen, the per-company spend of PSUs was approximately thirteen times that of non-PSUs. Even taking into account that many PSUs are much larger than private companies, the amount of contribution by PSUs to development is significant.

Box 4.4: Public Sector to the Fore—Powergrid Corporation

Corporate Award for Excellence in CSR in the Category: CSR Spend above Rs 100 Crore

The CSR activities of Powergrid Corporation, one of India's large PSUs, span from healthcare to education and skill development, to rural development, water-sanitation, and ecology and environment. All the activities aim to benefit mainly the marginalized and weaker sections of the population, including in remote and far-flung rural areas spread across the country.

Their project 'Improving Rural Livelihoods through Integrated Watershed Management' was the winner of the Government of India's Ministry of Corporate Affairs' topmost CSR award. Through the project, about 12,500 hectares of land in the semi-arid districts of Kurnool (in Andhra Pradesh) and Vijayapura (erstwhile Bijapur) (in

Karnataka) were taken up for watershed development in association with the International Crops Research Institute for the Semi-Arid Tropics (ICRISAT). The initiative created water storage capacity of about 95,000 m^3 which led to conservation of about 145,000 m^3 of run-off water. The groundwater table improved, and this led to improved crop productivity, resulting in increased incomes for over 10,000 farmers.

Based on: https://www.powergrid.in/csr/key-csr-activities

With such traditions in both the public and private sectors, CSR is an integral part of the thinking of Indian businesses. Its shape and manifestation continuously evolve, responding to the times.

Box 4.5: New Philanthropy

Mark Sidel (2000) refers to a phenomenon he calls 'Bengaluru philanthropy' (because Bengaluru-based IT companies have typically led the phenomenon). This is the philanthropy of the new-economy companies. This type of philanthropy is led by individual first-generation entrepreneurs who have created their wealth themselves and therefore are not shackled by family pressures on how much they may give to social causes, nor are they bound by family traditions on what to support and how.

How did we get to Section 135 of the Companies Act, 2013?

As we have seen, India has a long-standing tradition of CSR, which had been growing organically over the decades. With Companies Act, 2013, coming into effect on 1 April 2014, the country saw a paradigm shift in the evolutionary path of CSR. Mandating CSR had no precedent in any large country of the world. Hence it would be interesting to briefly explore how we got to this point.

It was a journey that spanned several years. Raghunathan M.L. (2017) tracks it as described in this section. The revamping of the law governing companies was in discussion much before the Companies Act, 2013, was legislated. The Parliamentary Standing Committee on Finance submitted its twenty-first report on the draft Companies Bill, 2009. It mentioned its concern over the lack of focus among corporates on CSR, and recommended that there be a policy on this. The Committee recommended that provisions regarding CSR be included in the Bill, and that CSR disclosures be made by companies in their annual reports. In reaction to this, the Ministry of Corporate Affairs expressed a view that a CSR spend of 2 per cent of profits of the last three years be made mandatory for companies meeting certain net worth/ turnover/profit criteria.

Probably the first official document which was devoted to the social responsibility of business was the *Corporate Social Responsibility Voluntary Guidelines* brought out in 2009 by the Ministry of Corporate Affairs.

The then-Minister for corporate affairs, Salman Khurshid, in his foreword to the 2009 document clarifies why the government had become seriously concerned about the environmental and social responsibilities of businesses. He notes that the rapid growth of the private sector and the financial crisis which had hit the world had led to a situation where industry was faced with only two options—inclusive growth or unsustainability. The minister opined that in popular perception, corporate growth was leading to increasing disparities, and therefore, there was increasing need for industry to demonstrate socially responsible business practices. As he put it, 'The business sector also needs to take the responsibility of exhibiting socially responsible business practices that ensure the distribution of wealth and the well-being of the communities in which the business operates.' (Ministry of Corporate Affairs, 2009)

The *Guidelines* clearly state that 'CSR is not philanthropy and the activities in the CSR guidelines are purely voluntary', and requests businesses to embrace the guidelines with enthusiasm. It lays down a framework of what socially responsible business practices are, and suggests that companies should draw up CSR policies covering six core elements, namely:

1. Care for all stakeholders,
2. Ethical functioning,
3. Respect for workers' rights and welfare,
4. Respect for human rights,
5. Respect for the environment, and
6. Activities for social and inclusive development.

Box 4.6: Success Driven by Stakeholder Focus

The TVS Group founded in 1911 is driven by a deep philosophy of responsibility to all stakeholders—employees, customers, community, and the environment.

Their focus on employees is exemplified by the section of TVS Motor Company's vision which states that: 'TVS Motor will create an enabling ambience where the maximum self-actualisation of every employee is achieved. TVS Motor will support and encourage the process of self-renewal in all its employees and nurture their sense of self-worth' (www.tvsmotor.com).

It is perhaps because of this commitment that a media report on the Group's centenary called it a '100-year old group with a unique achievement—it has never faced a serious labour problem' (Madhavan, 2011).

The report further goes on to mention how during the market meltdown of 2008, the TVS management felt the need for a temporary cut in workers' wages. But rather than doing it top-down, they decided to let the workers decide how much cut they would take. Not only did the workers agree to a wage cut, but suggested a 15 per cent cut—three times what the management was expecting (ibid.).

The 2009 document was followed by the *National Voluntary Guidelines on Social, Environmental & Economic Responsibilities of Business* (NVG for short), brought out in July 2011 by the same Ministry. This document takes into account the importance of the Triple Bottom Line (people, planet, and profit).

The NVG document seeks to be open and provide flexibility. It is not prescriptive, but rather cites examples of best practices of business responsibility as exemplars. It suggests processes and frameworks, rather than mandating anything. It mentions that medium and small-scale industries, which are such a significant part of Indian industry, need to follow these guidelines. The NVG lays down nine 'Principles of Responsible Business'. In spirit, these are close to the 2009 document, but they are wider than it (Ministry of Corporate Affairs, 2011). The nine principles are as follows:

1. Businesses should conduct and govern themselves with ethics, transparency, and accountability.
2. Businesses should provide goods and services that are safe and contribute to sustainability throughout their life cycle.
3. Businesses should promote the well-being of all employees.
4. Businesses should respect the interests of, and be responsive towards all stakeholders, especially those who are disadvantaged, vulnerable, and marginalized.
5. Businesses should respect and promote human rights.
6. Businesses should respect, protect, and make effort to restore the environment.
7. Businesses, when engaged in influencing public and regulatory policy, should do so in a responsible manner.
8. Businesses should support inclusive growth and equitable development.
9. Businesses should engage with and provide value to their customers and consumers in a responsible manner.

In 2010, then-Secretary, Ministry of Corporate Affairs (MCA), R. Bandopadhyay in conversation with Jitendra V. Singh, then professor of management at Wharton, said that '[the] Ministry and the Government have a responsibility towards investors and the general public' (Singh, 2010). Their discussion contains many insights into the evolution and thinking behind these guidelines. Elaborating on why they have been kept as just guidelines and not manadated by law, Secretary Bandopadhyay explained:

> MCA doesn't want to make something which is absolutely codified and becomes a part of law so that you [have to] follow it. If you don't follow it then you are punished. We don't want to do that in the beginning. We have given the best guidelines, evolved over time, telling companies to adopt as many guidelines and as many clauses as possible that are suitable for their company. For genuine reasons you may not be able to implement fully all these guidelines. You comply as much as possible. Where you cannot comply you give an explanation—an explanation not to the Ministry but to your shareholders, to your Board (ibid.).

However, he mentions that this was an initial step and that the Ministry would be reviewing the experience before deciding whether these should remain as guidelines to be followed voluntarily, or be mandated by law.

In 2012, when the Companies Bill, 2011 (later passed as the Companies Act, 2013) was being drafted, the then Union Minister for Corporate Affairs, Veerappa Moily, speaking at the first National CSR Conclave, reiterated that CSR should not be seen as philanthropy but rather a, 'symbiotic relationship with the environment in which a corporation operates'. He mentioned that CSR had to go beyond donations. In fact, even seeing CSR as 'risk-mitigating investments in community development' was a limited view. Rather, it should be seen as 'new ways to do core business differently, with inclusion as a driving force' (ibid.). He made the strong statement that 'stakeholders in a responsible business transcend the shareholders' (ibid.).

Making the case for CSR in a society with huge economic disparities, Moily said that the government had not mandated the spend of 2 per cent profit, because it was not in favour of forcing its views on the private sector (ibid.). However, he mentioned that the suggestion that such a spend be made had been placed in the draft of the Companies Bill, 2011, as a step towards providing a proper regulatory framework that enabled corporates to freely unleash entrepreneurship, at the same time making their contribution to inclusive growth and national development.

While the Companies Bill was still under discussion, SEBI, vide its circular dated 13 August 2012, made it mandatory for the 100 largest companies, to include a Business Responsibility Report (BRR) as part of their annual reports. The BRR format was based on the NVG framework. A few years later in 2015, SEBI approved a resolution to increase the coverage from the top 100 to the top 500 firms.

Raghunathan M.L. (2017) points out that the direction of thinking in India till this time is more or less on the same lines as the international thinking on the subject. She points out the similarity of the NVGs to the UN Global Compact which, as we have seen, urges businesses worldwide to adopt, practise, and report their sustainability and social responsibility practices. The NVG are more contextualized to India, but they draw on the UNGC principles.

And then…

And then in 2013, when the Companies Act was passed, this landmark legislation overhauled and brought up-to-date the legal regimen governing every aspect of the conduct of business by companies. Section 135 and Schedule VII, which shaped the understanding and operationalization of CSR in India from this point onwards, generated much discussion.

After the passage of the Act, on 27 February 2014, the Ministry of Corporate Affairs went on to notify the Companies Rules under Section 135 of the Act. These Rules came into force from 1 April 2014. Over the next few years, further addendums and clarifications were issued from time to time, not so much altering the basic elements, but more towards clearing doubts and grey areas. In September 2020 however, major amendments related to CSR were brought about. This was followed by another set of amendments on 22 January 2021. Both these sets of amendments brought about significant changes.

At this stage, it is relevant to flag that the law with regard to CSR is still evolving and different clauses are being modified based on feedback from time to time. Changes/clarifications are brought out frequently, which need to be tracked by CSR-related professionals. We will be discussing the details of the law and operational aspects in subsequent chapters.

Reasons behind Mandating CSR in India

Why did the Government of India take this drastic step of mandating CSR? All definitions and all scholars agree that at the core of CSR is the voluntary nature of the activity and 'going beyond the law'. As we have seen, the government's initial thought process was not to mandate CSR. It was expected to remain voluntary. But the thinking changed over the years that the new company law was under discussion.

Raghunathan, M.L. (2017) sums up the reasons put forward by many thinkers and practitioners as to why this might have been done. Some scholars opined that India, as a socialistic country had always had a focus on increasing economic equity; but the fruits of economic development did not trickle down quite as envisaged, and inequities continued to increase. India's poor performance on the HDI and its deteriorating environment—both of which remained matters of concern—may also have contributed significantly to the logic behind the legislation to make CSR mandatory.

Other scholars, she mentions, see the Act as a move which achieved two objectives simultaneously—it demonstrated the government's seriousness about strengthening social welfare measures (a step which would please the public), while at the same time not imposing tax increases on businesses towards social welfare (thus making businesses happy). At the same time, the suggested process gave businesses flexibility on how they wished to make this spend. The government might have felt that the law would help to achieve better environmental and social sustainability. Maybe the thinking took root that purely voluntary initiatives would never be taken up enthusiastically by businesses. Thus, mandating it was probably seen as a systemic way of making corporates share responsibility for overall socio-economic development.

It must be borne in mind that the law took shape at a time when there was a negative perception about big business in general. It was indeed becoming difficult for some of them to operate as social licence was not easily forthcoming from communities and society. It might have been felt that mandating CSR would force companies to recognize and do something about their responsibilities to their communities. Once tangible benefits were seen by the community it would result in a healthier environment for business. Maybe that is why this law encourages businesses to carry out CSR activities in their neighbourhoods.

There might also have been a perception that such a move could reduce the criticism that governments cared more for business than for the well-being of communities.

Some scholars like Shachi Rai and Sangeeta Bansal (2015) suggest that one reason could have been the government's perception that philanthropic activities of corporates needed to be more accountable and transparent. A decade ago, there were many companies doing CSR, but decisions on the shape, scope and scale were taken by each individual company. The government might have seen the law as a way to streamline and direct these spends towards national priorities.

Yet another explanation could be that perhaps it was hoped that the corporate sector would bring its execution efficiency and systematic management approaches to social development through CSR. While making CSR compulsory, the financial resources it would bring in might have been only a minor consideration with the government. The calculation at the time the law was mandated was that total mandatory CSR spend was going to be less than 2 per cent of the government's spending on the social sector, and hence would not significantly affect social development programmes or outcomes.

Hence it may be concluded that the government's rationale to make CSR mandatory was a push to make the corporate sector take more responsibility and to inculcate the spirit of community development and inclusive growth.

The two statements which ran as a ticker tape on the official CSR website (www.csr.gov.in) as of March 2022, may provide an insight into the current perspective on CSR:

> Successful companies have a social responsibility to make the world a better place and not just take from it. CSR extends beyond Corporate Philanthropy.
>
> It is a collective responsibility to build a society which supplements Government's efforts to achieve inclusive growth which includes broad-based benefits and ensures equality of opportunity for all.

Box 4.7: Not Common at All...

One may wonder if any other country in the world has mandated CSR. Well, there are a few examples. China's 2006 company law for example, requires that 'in the course of doing business, a company shall comply with laws and administrative regulations, conform to social morality and business ethics, act in good faith, subject itself to the government and the public supervision, and undertake social responsibility (Li-Wen Lin 2019). Indonesia's law, of the same vintage, declares that companies 'can set aside some part of their net profit to develop the small business/koperasi and development of society surrounding government business organization', and that 'Social and environment responsibilities are an obligation for each corporation which is budgeted and calculated as corporate expenses which is fair and proper'(ibid).

However the only other exemplar of mandatory CSR, in terms of legally specifying a minimum threshold of spend and articulating consequences of non-compliance, is Mauritius. It was probably the first country to mandate corporates to spend on CSR. As in India, there too, CSR-related provisions have undergone many modifications.

As per Ah-Hen (2016) the first reference to CSR in Mauritius came in their 2009 Income Tax Act, wherein all profitable firms were required to spend 2 per cent of book profits towards CSR activities under six specified programme areas, and following government-mandated means of implementation. In 2010, focus areas were brought down to three national priorities. In 2012, came the amendment that the 2 per cent contribution be calculated on the basis of 'profit chargeable to income tax' and a fourth programme area was included. In 2015, the norms were relaxed and companies were asked to spend as per their priorities. There were again changes in 2016–17 under which:

1. A National CSR Foundation to undertake, monitor, serve as a CSR platform was set up.
2. Six priority areas were specified.
3. It was made mandatory for companies to contribute at least 50 per cent of their CSR fund to the Foundation. They were also asked to give any amount remaining unspent at the end of the year to the Foundation.

Reactions to Mandating CSR

The final draft of the Companies Act was in discussion through 2012 and 2013 in India. It was a comprehensive overhaul of an old and outdated Act governing all aspects of the setting up and running of companies. The Act, in its final shape, has 466 working sections dealing with everything from the incorporation of companies to issue of share capital, to appointment of a Board of directors. But of all the provisions, the section that caught the public imagination and was most discussed and debated was probably Section 135 on CSR!

Many points of view were put forward on mandatory CSR in this phase, before the Companies Act was legislated. One of the most serious criticisms was that equating CSR to a mandated spend on some causes would actually take away from the effort of getting companies to proactively integrate social and environmental responsibility into the making of their core business decisions.

From an economic perspective, it was criticized on the grounds that if CSR made economic sense in the short and long terms, companies would themselves have taken it up. Others felt that the total size of the mandated spend was inconsequential, given that it was probably going to be less than 2 per cent of the government's spending on the social sector, and hence not worth all the trouble.

Those with leanings to the left felt that government was reneging on its responsibilities by mandating CSR and trying to get businesses to do what it should be doing. They felt that the better option would have been for the government to raise corporate taxes and spend the money as per their priorities, rather than leave CSR actions to individual corporates. Those with leanings to the right felt that making spending compulsory was equivalent to raising corporate taxes (already high in India) by a further 2 per cent, which would make India less competitive in the global market. Those in the centre objected, saying that CSR was not something to be mandated but rather something to be driven by individual corporate motivations—corporate social responsibility ought not to become corporate legal liability. Some scholars were also concerned about the overwhelming responsibility, discretion, and power given to corporate Boards.

There were however those who thought that the proposed legislation was a good move, as such a move would result not only in community development but also lead to better operational efficiencies, environmental management, and new models of creating shared value. Such community initiatives would help to reduce the friction between communities and corporates and result in a win-win situation, with community benefits *and* sustainability for the corporate. It was also opined that since 2 per cent was not too high a proportion, corporates would not find it difficult to set aside this fraction from their profits for these activities.

The law as adopted in 2014 required certain categories of companies to spend 2 per cent of their profits, but if they failed to do so, they only had to give reasons for this. This aspect of the law was appreciated—that it did not seek to penalize, but rather, laid out a 'comply or explain' regime, where the Board was responsible for meeting CSR commitments, but if it had a good reason for not meeting these, it needed only to share the reasons thereof with the authorities and stakeholders. As opposed to the 'comply or else' approach, it was felt that the mandated process left some amount of discretion with the highest decision-making body of the corporate, viz., the Board. The flexibility of the government allowing various channels for spending was appreciated, as it made it possible even for firms without their own CSR staff and structures to comply. Since no formal monitoring mechanism was proposed by the government, it was opined that the law was being brought in from government's desire to push corporates towards voluntary spending with mandatory reporting.

However, since 2014, we have seen many changes in the various requirements and processes. The consequences of not spending or underspending have been viewed increasingly seriously. At one stage, such infractions were even being regarded as criminal offences. Though the criminality of these breaches was subsequently removed, any underspending has not only to be reported, but depending on the circumstances, the amounts have to be carried over or contributed to certain funds, and spent over subsequent years, and there are fines.

Stringent and detailed reporting formats have also been put into place. There definitely are repercussions for not complying!

Impacts of Mandating CSR

Following the law coming into force, there has been wide and increasing compliance and spending by companies.

Research by Sarkar and Sarkar (2015) sets a context. They found that in 2003 only 7 per cent of the 500 biggest firms had carried out and reported CSR activity (of course, many may have done CSR but not reported it). By 2011, about 62 per cent firms were doing both. This sharp increase is attributed to an increase in the number of companies undertaking or increasing CSR activities in the heightened CSR-supportive environment. It is thought that this might have been their effort to demonstrate their willingness to voluntarily undertake CSR, in order to prevent it being made mandatory.

The increase may also have been because many companies, hitherto undertaking but not reporting CSR, started to report it. However, many firms—which post-2014 would come under the purview of the law—continued not incurring any CSR spend.

Trends in CSR Spending

The following healthy trends are seen in CSR-related data from the Ministry of Corporate Affairs in the period following the enactment of the law. The data discussed below mainly confine themselves to the period 2014–20, as spends for 2020–21 are not truly reflective of trends for many COVID-related reasons, including the falling of profits due to the pandemic-related disruption, the inability of some companies which needed to spend being unable to do so due to either cash constraints or operational challenges, and much higher spending by some companies than mandated to support Covid-related relief programmes.

Total Amount Spent

As per the Ministry of Corporate Affairs (www.mca.gov.in), based on reports filed till January 2016, in FY 2014–15, the first year of the operation of the law, only about 30 per cent of mandated companies reported that they had spent any amount on CSR, and in all about 74 per cent of the calculated mandatory spend amount was actually spent. In FY 2019–20, about 66 per cent had spent as much or more than the sums mandated for them, showing a healthy trend of compliance (www.csr.gov.in).

Figure 4.1: CSR spend (in Rs crore) from 2014–15 to 2019–20

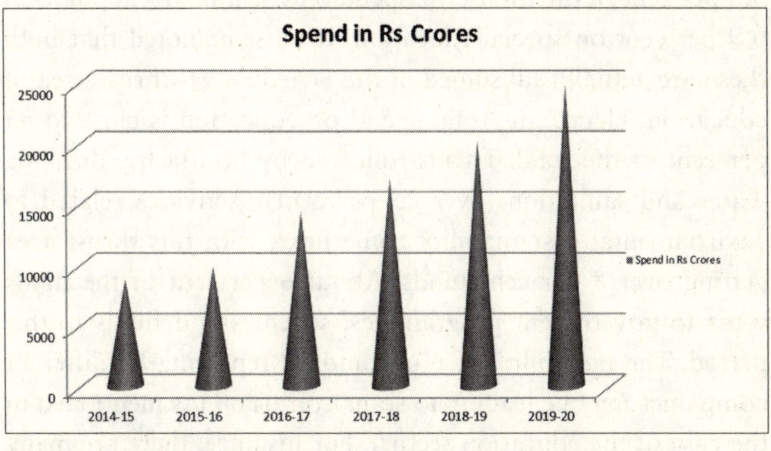

Source: Data from www.csr.gov.in, retrieved 14 March 2022

On the whole, both spends and compliance have been increasing steadily and corporates seem to have embraced the mandate, seeing CSR as an opportunity to participate and contribute to the country's development. The cumulative amount spent is estimated to be a little short of Rs 1,00,000 crore in the first six years of the CSR provisions coming into force (i.e., from FY 2014–15 to 2019–20). Even in the old regime which did not have punitive consequences for non-spending, it was anticipated that compliance would be close to 100 per cent by FY 2020–21 or 2021–22. While Covid has been a disruptor, with stringent consequences being brought in, this figure is sure to be reached soon.

Thrust Areas

As per government data, the education sector received the maximum funding (about 30 per cent) in this six-year period (see Figure 4.2). In addition to this, figures show a spending of 3.5 per cent of the total CSR spend on vocational training, and 0.9 per cent on special education. It must be noted that both these are actually subsumed in the Schedule VII thrust area of education. Hence, the total spend on education is close to 35 per cent of the total. This is followed by healthcare, drinking water and sanitation (over 25 per cent). Activities related to environmental sustainability come next, with this thrust area getting over 8 per cent funds. About 6 per cent of the funds went to government programmes, schemes and funds in this period. The possibility of non-standard reporting by different companies may be leading to some confusion (as mentioned in the case of the education sector). For instance, there are many initiatives directed towards the health of senior citizens. Some companies may report these under 'healthcare', whereas others may do so under 'senior citizen welfare'. Similarly, there may be overlaps between 'slum development' and 'addressing socio-economic inequalities'.

What can clearly be seen however is that funding to causes like orphanages, or activities like technology incubators and sports, remains low. Something which is not easily explainable is that about 3.2 per cent of the CSR spend is reported to have been in activities whose thrust areas have not been mentioned. As the reporting formats make it very difficult not to mention thrust areas, it is not very clear where the spend is going, or why and how it is not reported.

Figure 4.2: Six-year CSR spend on key thrust areas (Rs crore)

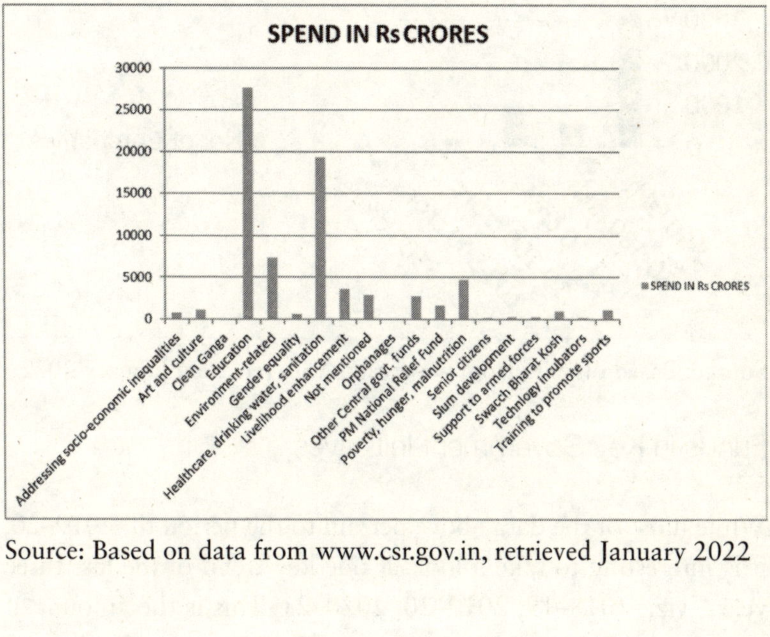

Source: Based on data from www.csr.gov.in, retrieved January 2022

Spend SIze

About 60 per cent companies have a CSR spend of Rs 50 lakh or less; only thirty-seven companies spent over Rs 100 crore in 2019–20 (see Figure 4.3). Energy and resource companies, financial services, and information technology services, have been among the highest spenders. In terms of listed and unlisted companies, about 78 per cent of the CSR spend is by unlisted companies.

Figure 4.3: CSR spend size (Rs) 2019-20

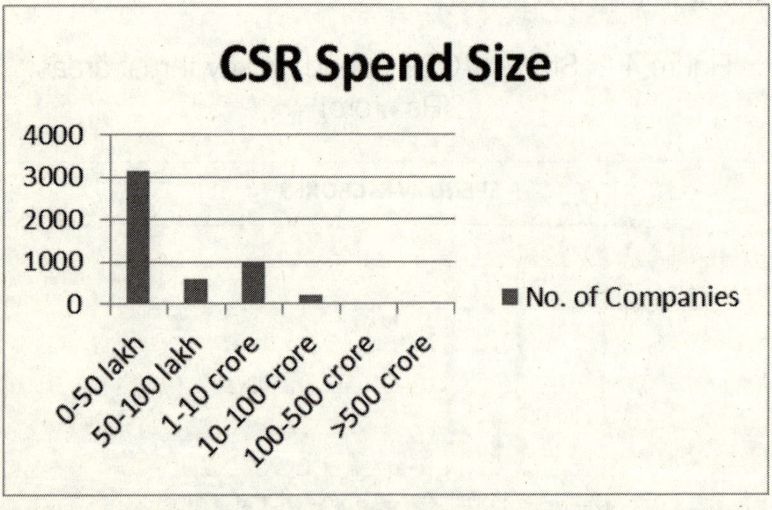

Source: Based on data from www.csr.gov.in, retrieved January 2022

Funds in Key Government Initiatives

While most of the data above pertain to the period till 2019–20, it is interesting to take a look at one key trend of the last three years, viz., 2018–19, 2019–20, 2020–21. This is the amount of CSR funds going into key government initiatives (see Table 4.1).

Table 4.1: CSR funds (Rs crore) in key government initiatives

Scheme	2018–19	2019–20	2020–21
Clean Ganga Fund	8	6	7
PM National Relief Fund	320	796	1,452
Swachh Bharat Kosh	95	53	148
Any other funds	730	930	1,327
Total	1,153	1,785	2,934

Source: Based on data from www.csr.gov.in, retrieved March 2022

Different people have different explanations for this. One set opines that corporates perceive some pressure to contribute to these funds, and this was especially marked during the Covid pandemic. Others say that many companies find the implementation protocols complex and compliance risks high. They find contributing to these funds much easier on both these fronts. It must also be mentioned that in the first two years or so of the law coming in, the contributions to government funds was high, which was mainly because companies had not yet set up their implementation mechanisms. In the intervening years, these contributions had dipped, but now are again on a rising trend.

Covid has had a disruptive effect on CSR spends and the impacts are likely to be long-term. With the pandemic striking towards the end of FY 2019–20, some amount of funds had already started to go towards this challenge in 2019–20 itself. The start of FY 2020–21 continued to see efforts in this direction—from supporting migrants to donating personal protective equipment (PPE kits), to health-related efforts. In fact, the year 2020–21 saw a 30 per cent increase in healthcare spends, and a decrease in spends on education, environment, and sustainability (India Philanthropy Report 2022).

There were considerable contributions to the PM Cares Fund too, especially after this was included in the list of eligible CSR activities. While there is no authentic source which gives information on how much CSR funding went into this program, it is thought to be very significant. While profits of FY 2019–20, and hence mandatory CSR spend amounts for FY 2020–21, were not impacted significantly Covid notwithstanding, with the serious second wave, business in FY 2020–21 has been seriously affected, and this would significantly reduce the CSR fund availability in the coming few years.

Most field activities, whether education or rural development, were in pause mode for close to two years. There are now new challenges with regard to education, livelihoods, health, etc.

What is certain is that the world has changed, and CSR programmes are being reconceived and reimagined to address the emerging socio-economic challenges. It will require innovation and creative thinking on the part of social development professionals to design innovative and impactful CSR programmes for these times.

Box 4.8: Topping the Charts

The top ten spenders list for 2020–21 represents a good mix of public and private sector enterprises. Several IT and resource companies find a place in the list. The first in the list was Reliance Industries, with a spend of Rs 922 crore, followed by Tata Consultancy Services (TCS), Tata Sons, HDFC Bank, Oil and Natural Gas Corporation Ltd (ONGC), Indian Oil Corporation Ltd (IOC), NTPC Ltd, Infosys, ITC Ltd, and Wipro.

Based on https://www.csr.gov.in

5

Operationalizing the Law: Comply or...

As we have seen, on 1 April 2014, India became the first major country in the world to bring into force mandatory CSR through Section 135 of the Companies Act, 2013. Since then, the law has been amended, and new rules brought in several times, the latest being the significant changes brought in on 22 January 2021. The law applies to all companies in India which fulfil certain criteria of net worth, turnover, and net profit, whether they are listed or unlisted, in the public sector or private sector.

It is important for stakeholders—starting with Board and CSR committee members to CEOs, CFOs, company secretaries, and auditors, to CSR leaders and staff, to NGOs and other implementing agencies—to not only understand the nuances of the law, but also keep track of changes.

In this chapter, the effort will be to give an overview of critical compliance-related clauses, in order to gain operational clarity. This said, it is also necessary to mention that in any case of confusion or lack of clarity, it is best to refer the question to a specialist for interpretation. Before going into the parts, let us look at the landmark Section 135 in its original form. The operational details of the law and amendments will be discussed subsequently.

The Original Landmark CSR Mandate

(1) 'Every company having net worth of rupees five hundred crore or more, or turnover of rupees one thousand crore or more or a net profit of rupees five crore or more during any financial year shall constitute a Corporate Social Responsibility Committee of the Board* consisting of three or more directors, of which at least one shall be an independent director.

(2) The Board's report under sub-section (3) of section 134 shall disclose the composition of the Corporate Social Responsibility Committee.

(3) The Corporate Social Responsibility Committee* shall,—

a. Formulate and recommend to the Board, a Corporate Social Responsibility Policy which shall indicate the activities to be undertaken by the company as specified in Schedule VII;
b. recommend the amount of expenditure to be incurred on the activities referred to in clause (a); and
c. monitor the Corporate Social Responsibility Policy of the company from time to time.

(4) The Board of every company referred to in sub-section (1) shall, —
formulate and recommend to the Board, a Corporate Social Responsibility Policy which shall indicate the activities to be undertaken by the company as specified in Schedule VII;

a. after taking into account the recommendations made by the Corporate Social Responsibility Committee, approve the Corporate Social Responsibility Policy for the company and disclose contents of such Policy in its report and also place it on the company's website, if any, in such manner as may be prescribed; and
b. ensure that the activities as included in Corporate Social Responsibility Policy of the company are undertaken by the company.

(5) The Board of every company referred to in sub-section (1), shall ensure that the company spends, in every financial year, at least two per cent of the average net profits of the Company made during the three immediately preceding financial years,in pursuance of its Corporate Social Responsibility Policy:**
Provided that the company shall give preference to the local area and areas around it where it operates, for spending the amount earmarked for Corporate Social Responsibility activities:
Provided further that if the company fails to spend such amount, the Board shall, in its report made under clause (o) of sub-section (3) of section 134, specify the reasons for not spending the amount.'***

Explanation—For the purposes of this section "average net profit" shall be calculated in accordance with the provisions of section 198.'

*, **, *** : Key amendments have been made with regard to these, which will be discussed further on.

(From: https://mca.gov.in/)

Box 5.1: Mandatory CSR and the Public Sector

Government of India mandates have explicitly laid down the specifics of CSR implementation of Central Public Sector Enterprises (CPSEs). The government came out with its *Guidelines for Corporate Social Responsibility in Central Public Sector Enterprises* in 2007, which specified mandated spend on CSR in terms of percentage of profits of the previous year (3–5 per cent for less than Rs 100 crore profit; 2–3 per cent for Rs 100 to 500 crore; and 0.5–2 per cent for more than Rs 500 crore). More importantly, the government came out with processes, systems, and suggestions on how they could effectively implement CSR, including what activities could be undertaken, how they could be planned, implemented, monitored, etc.

For public sector units traditionally in the forefront of CSR, new guidelines were enacted in 2013, following the new Companies Act. After the enactment of the new company law, it has been clarified that the provisions of Section 135 of the Act and Schedule VII of the Act

(CSR Rules) apply to all companies, including CPSEs. In addition to this, the Department of Public Enterprises (DPE) formulated *Guidelines on CSR and Sustainability* which are applicable to CPSEs. The DPE *Guidelines* do not supersede or override any provision of the Act, or Schedule VII of the Act, or the CSR Rules, but only supplement them. It has been clarified that in case of perceived conflict between the CSR Rules and the DPE *Guidelines*, the former shall prevail in all circumstances

In their CSR policies, CPSEs are also required to include a vision and mission statement of how they propose to comply with the *Guidelines*. The CSR requirement for such enterprises is even more stringent than for private sector companies, because the DPE *Guidelines* state that even those companies which are not covered under the eligibility criteria based on the threshold limits of net worth, turnover, or net profit as specified by Section 135 (1) of the Act, but which made profit in the preceding year, would also be required to take up CSR activities as specified in the Act and the CSR Rules, and such CPSEs would be expected to spend at least 2 per cent of the profit made in the preceding year on CSR activities. The requirement to carry over the unspent amount, which was made compulsory for the private sector only in 2021, has been a requirement for the public sector for several years now. The new mandate for CPSEs is to spend a significant part of their CSR funds in aspirational districts, with specific themes each year.

Based on www.https://dpe.gov.in/dpe-guidelines/corporate-social-responsibility

Operationalizing the Law

The sub-sections under this section will take up each of the key clauses and discuss operational implications and aspects. Most of the discussion is in the context of the private sector, as the guidelines for the public sector are a little different, and are covered in Box 5.1 above. (There may be some additional compliances for foreign companies.)

Companies in the Purview of the Law

Does the mandatory CSR provision apply to all companies in India? Well, here is one question which can be answered unequivocally, with a clear 'No'.

The mandatory CSR provision is applicable to larger companies, defined as those which in the immediately preceding financial year touched

- Net worth of Rs 500 crore or more, or
- Turnover of Rs 1,000 crore or more, or
- Net profit of Rs 5 crore.

(Interestingly, the CSR mandate applies only to corporate entities incorporated under the Companies Act, 2013. Entities registered as Limited Liability Partnerships [LLPs] or public sector banks are left out of the purview, as they are governed by different laws—the LLP Act, 2008, and the Banking Regulation Act, 1949. The government is said to be contemplating mechanisms to bring these under the CSR mandate too.)

The important point to note here is that a company which falls into any one of these criteria falls within the ambit of the provisions. This provision kicks into play as soon as the company meets any one of these criteria, however young or old the company may be. Companies falling within the purview of the law must take the following actions.

Constitute a CSR Committee of the Board

While this used to be mandatory for all companies falling under the purview of the law, an amendment brought about in September 2020 states this requirement is not applicable if the mandatory spend is less than Rs 50 lakh, and the Board can carry out the functions of the CSR committee. The company must disclose the composition of the committee where there is one.

The composition of the CSR Committee is also laid down for different types of companies. For instance, the Committee of a listed company must have at least three members, at least one of whom is an independent director. It is similar for unlisted public companies, except that if there is no requirement to have an independent director, this is waived for the CSR Committee as well. (General Circular No. 14, 21 August 2021 has details for other types of companies; see Ministry of Corporate Affairs, 2021).

On a practical note, since the mandatory CSR amount varies from year to year, unless a company is sure that it will not exceed Rs 50 lakh in the foreseeable future, it is probably wise to constitute a CSR committee anyway. Such sub-committees of the Board should ideally not be constituted and dissolved frequently.

What the CSR Committee Needs to Do

The CSR Committee is required to

- Formulate and recommend a CSR policy to the Board,
- From year-to-year, based on the calculations of the CSR spend for the year, discuss and recommend annual plans and budgets (based on the policy), to the Board,

- Monitor the implementation of the plans from time to time,
- Meet twice a year and make recommendations to the Board, and
- Recommend any changes to the annual plan during the year.

Board's Responsbility

In case the spend is less than Rs 50 lakh, and the company does not have a CSR Committee, the Board has to take up the above responsibilities, in addition to the ones listed below:

- Discuss and approve the CSR policy;
- Discuss and approve recommendations made by the CSR Committee with regard to budgets, activities, and changes in plans, etc;
- Ensure disclosure of contents of such policy in its report, and also placing the policy and projects on the company's website;
- Ensure that the policy is adhered to, and activities as included in CSR policy of the company are undertaken by it;
- Satisfy itself with regard to the utilization of the amount as per the provisions of the law, and as approved by it;
- Ensure that the administrative overheads do not exceed 5 per cent of the spend at company level;
- In case of ongoing projects (i.e., those spanning more than one financial year), assure itself that the initiative is going as per plan, timelines, and budgets;
- Approve the claiming of credit of CSR overspending in any one year, over the subsequent three years;
- Ensure that the report of the Board of directors carries a CSR annual report as per required format;
- Ensure that impact assessment is done as per the law, review these reports and ensure that the same are included in the CSR annual report;

- Give details and specify reason in its report, in case the company does not spend the required amount; also approve the transfer of the unspent amount as per the relevant legal provisions and include all these in the required format in the CSR annual report.

It must be mentioned here that CSR compliance is company-specific. In other words, with respect to a group of companies, a holding or subsidiary company does not come under the purview of the law, unless it comes under one of the criteria itself.

It may also be noted that all companies—whether listed or unlisted—need to comply with the law. The government has even clarified that Section 8 (not-for-profit companies) fall within the purview of the law, though it is not quite clear what the CSR spend calculation will be in such cases, as these are based on profits.

Does every company falling in the purview of the law have to undertake CSR activity and spend? The simple answer is 'No'. As mentioned before, while the provision is applicable to all large companies (as defined earlier in the section), simply falling under one of these criteria does not mean that the company has to undertake CSR activities or spends.

For a company to compulsorily undertake a CSR spend, in addition to falling within one of the three criteria cited above, its average net profits during the three immediately preceding financial years must also be positive. This implies that a large company that has net losses over the preceding three years does not have any mandatory spend.

So does it mean that such a company, with negative average profits over three years, is free from all statutory obligations vis-à-vis CSR? Not really. Any company which falls in any of the three criteria mentioned above, irrespective of its profits, still has to take most of the actions described earlier in the section.

These are repeated here, with the actions for zero mandatory spends highlighted.

- The Board has to formulate and approve a CSR policy indicating the CSR activities (in a case where there is no spend for the year, the policy must still be recommended, indicating the thrust areas of activities as per Schedule VII, but no specific activities need to be mentioned).
- The Board must recommend the amount of expenditure to be incurred on the activities (in case of no spend as per the calculation, it may recommend zero spend and nil activities).
- The Board of every company needs to:
  - Discuss and approve the CSR policy;
  - Discuss and approve recommendations regarding budgets and activities;
  - Ensure disclosure of contents of such policy in its report and also place it on the company's website;
  - Make the necessary disclosures in the Board's report (mentioning that there is no mandatory CSR spend as per profit calculations, if this be the case);
  - Approve the claiming of credit of CSR overspending in any one year, over the subsequent three years, if there has been any in the previous years; and
  - Review the impact assessment reports of the initiatives for which these may be required, and ensure that the same are included in the CSR annual report, in case there was any mandatory impact assessment done for the previous years.

So effectively every large company as defined in Section 135 of the Companies Act, 2013, has to take many statutory actions, even if it does not have to undertake CSR activities or spend on CSR.

Going Beyond

Can a company incur CSR expenditure even if it does not have profits? And can it spend more than the mandated amount for a given year?

'Yes' is the answer to both questions. Any company, with the approval of its Board, can undertake CSR activities and incur CSR expenditure. In fact, January 2021 notification from the Ministry of Corporate Affairs enables companies to take credit for this by stipulating that:

> Provided also that if the company spends an amount in excess of the requirements provided under this sub-section, such company may set off such excess amount against the requirement to spend under this sub-section for such number of succeeding financial years and in such manner, as may be prescribed.

There is a specific reporting format for this within the annual report. It may be noted that credit for the excess amount can be claimed over the succeeding three years. If this is not done within three succeeding years, it will lapse.

Companies desiring to spend when they are not legally bound to, should still place their plans before the CSR Committee and/ or Board. Similar is the case of companies wanting to spend more than the mandated amount. Such situations are not rare. For instance, companies which have regular CSR projects going on over the years may find that they are suddenly on the cusp of three bad years when the three-year average profits are negative. But enlightened companies do not simply switch off their CSR spends even in such years.

And importantly, any company small or big, irrespective of whether it falls in the mandate or not, can undertake CSR. The mandate is only for the minimum!

Activities Counted as CSR as per the Law

Schedule VII of the Companies Act, 2013, lays down what counts as CSR in India. The good news is that the gamut is wide and the framework flexible. To quote Schedule VII, the following are deemed eligible CSR activities:

(i) Eradicating hunger, poverty and malnutrition, promoting health care including preventive health care and sanitation [including contribution to the Swach Bharat Kosh set up by the Central Government for the promotion of sanitation] and making available safe drinking water;

(ii) promoting education, including special education and employment enhancing vocation skills especially among children, women, elderly and the differently abled and livelihood enhancement projects;

(iii) promoting gender equality, empowering women, setting up homes and hostels for women and orphans; setting up old age homes, day care centres and such other facilities for senior citizens and measures for reducing inequalities faced by socially and economically backward groups;

(iv) ensuring environmental sustainability, ecological balance, protection of flora and fauna, animal welfare, agroforestry, conservation of natural resources and maintaining quality of soil, air and water [including contribution to the Clean

Ganga Fund set-up by the Central Government for rejuvenation of river Ganga];

(v) protection of national heritage, art and culture including restoration of buildings and sites of historical importance and works of art; setting up public libraries; promotion and development of traditional art and handicrafts;

(vi) measures for the benefit of armed forces veterans, war widows and their dependents, [Central Armed Police Forces (CAPF) and Central Para Military Forces (CPMF) veterans, and their dependents including widows];

(vii) training to promote rural sports, nationally recognised sports, sports and Olympic sports;

(viii) contribution to Funds currently specified in Schedule VII (a) Swachh Bharat Kosh; (b Clean Ganga Fund; (c) Prime Minister's National Relief Fund (PMNRF); (d) Prime Minister's Citizen Assistance and Relief in Emergency Situations Fund (PM CARES Fund); and (v) Any other fund set up by the Central Government and notified by the Ministry of Corporate Affairs, for socio-economic development and relief and welfare of the Scheduled Castes, the Scheduled Tribes, other backward classes, minorities and women;

(ix) contribution to incubators funded by Central Government or State Government or any agency or Public Sector Undertaking of Central Government or State Government, and contributions to public funded Universities, Indian Institute of Technology (IITs), National Laboratories and Autonomous Bodies (established under the auspices of Indian Council of Agricultural Research (ICAR), Indian

Council of Medical Research (ICMR), Council of Scientific and Industrial Research (CSIR), Department of Atomic Energy (DAE), Defence Research and Development Organisation (DRDO), [Department of Biotechnology (DBT)], Department of Science and Technology (DST), Ministry of Electronics and Information Technology) engaged in conducting research in science, technology, engineering and medicine aimed at promoting Sustainable Development Goals (SDGs);

(x) rural development projects;

(xi) slum area development;

(xii) disaster management, including relief, rehabilitation and reconstruction activities.

https://mca.gov.in/content/mca/global/en/acts-rules/

While the law clearly states that activities which do not fall under Schedule VII cannot be counted as CSR, it must be noted that this is an evolving list and it is useful to keep track of government announcements which come out from time to time, clarifications issued and amendments made. These either explain the scope of the provisions or add to them.

These provisions are very wide and it is possible to fit almost any CSR initiative into this framework. Also, the Ministry of Corporate Affairs has urged companies to interpret these provisions liberally while adhering to the spirit. The government has been flexible in expanding and elucidating this list to include more and more activities. For instance, the Ministry of Corporate Affairs clearly stated in its General Circular No. 21/2014 that 'the entries in the said Schedule VII must be interpreted liberally so as to capture the essence of the subjects enumerated' (Ministry of Corporate Affairs, 2014). In the same circular, it clarifies for instance that road safety programmes could be taken up as a part of the thrust area of promoting education, or if undertaken for professional drivers, under the thrust of vocational education.

There are often questions as to whether contribution to the corpus of an eligible organization would count as CSR expenditure. While this was allowed initially, in response to queries, the Ministry of Corporate Affairs clarified that contribution to the corpus would not qualify as CSR expenditure. As explained by the Ministry in its updated frequently asked questions (FAQs) released in August 2021, 'the provision relating to contribution to corpus as admissible CSR expenditure has been amended and the contribution to corpus of any entity is not an admissible CSR expenditure w.e.f. 22/01/2021' (Ministry of Corporate Affairs, 2021).

There have also been queries from time to time as to whether companies can donate their products or make in-kind contribution—e.g., software or medicines, as part of CSR. The law clearly says that to meet the CSR requirement, expenditure has to be incurred, and the latest clarifications reiterate that 'Therefore, CSR contribution cannot be in kind and monetized' (see Ministry of Corporate Affairs, 2021).

In other words, expenditure has to be incurred and booked. However, a court ruling in one instance has allowed the donation of medicines by a drug company to poor patients as CSR. In such a case, one presumes that there should be an actual sale and purchase, and therefore an expense. Even in this case, it is not clear whether the medicine cost is to be taken at market value or at cost to the corporate concerned. Moreover, care needs to be taken that the spirit of the law should not be violated, i.e., it should not be done in the spirit of distributing freebies or with an eye on profits—but with altruistic motives. Court judgment notwithstanding, it seems that it would be safer not to make this a significant part of the CSR activities.

Considering the matter from the angle of strategic CSR, this clause may actually prove to be a deterrent. For instance, similar in spirit to the donation of medicines by a pharma company, if a courier company wants to support the marketing efforts of women SHGs by offering them free or subsidized movement of their products, this cannot be accounted for as a CSR because of this clause.

As we shall see in the next section, a company cannot count 'activities undertaken in pursuance of normal course of business', as CSR. However, looking at the Covid emergency, an amendment has been brought in for a limited time period, as per which:

> Provided that any company engaged in research and development activity of new vaccine, drugs and medical devices in their normal course of business may undertake research and development activity of new vaccine, drugs and medical devices related to COVID-19 for financial years 2020–21, 2021–22 and 2022–23 subject to the conditions that such research and development activities shall be carried out in collaboration with any of the institutes or organisations mentioned in item (ix) of Schedule VII to the Act.
>
> The amendments also mention that in the said rules, in rule 4, sub-rule 1, the words "excluding activities undertaken in pursuance of its normal course of business" shall be omitted. The exact implications and scope of this will become clearer once the Rules are brought out.
>
> Ministry of Corporate Affairs notification no. G.S.R. 526(E), 24 August 2020

Activities not Counted as CSR as per the Law

The law not only lays down which activities count as CSR but also which do not. However, some of these clauses relating to what is not permissible are open to interpretation. If a company wants to venture into grey areas, it is better done with caution, and keeping in mind the spirit of the law. The provisions clarify that the following do not count towards the mandated CSR spend.

Projects or activities that benefit only employees and their families

While employees and their families can be 'incidental beneficiaries' of a company's CSR activities, no CSR activity can be designed to benefit employees. The spirit behind this is that CSR must benefit the larger public, and should be non-discriminatory.

There will be situations where these provisions may need to be interpreted. Consider a situation when a corporate runs a school on its premises. If the school is exclusively meant for the children of employees, it clearly will not count as CSR. If the school is open to children of employees as well as to fee-paying children from around, it is not clear if and to what extent it can count as CSR. However, if the school, besides taking in employees' children takes in other fee-paying children, and also has a provision for free education for underprivileged children, the last-mentioned expenditure may count towards the mandated spend. In such cases, it is always advisable to keep the spirit of the law as the guiding principle, and ensure that benefits commensurate with the spends claimed can be shown to be going to the general public, especially the socio-economically deprived.

During the Covid pandemic, some concessions were discussed in this clause for some specific activities like vaccination. It was thought that the government would allow vaccination for staff and families to be counted under CSR. However, it was later clarified that this would not be allowed.

Activities undertaken in pursuance of normal course of business of the company

If the core business of a company is to provide healthcare, rural infrastructure, skill development etc., it cannot count these activities as CSR. (As mentioned earlier, Covid-related R&D has been exempted for a specified time period).

One-off events

Events such as marathons, awards, charitable contribution, advertisement, sponsorships of TV programmes, etc. do not qualify as CSR. The spirit of this exclusion is clear. The objective of the CSR legislation is to nudge companies towards taking up long-term, outcome-oriented projects which improve the well-being of communities, and hence expenses on such one-time events are excluded from the mandated CSR spend. Often sponsorship of events is more in the nature of public relations and does not contribute to community development.

Such activities, if they are part of a strategic programme (and not one-off), may however be permitted. For instance, if a company decides to adopt an old age home in the vicinity of a factory and make charitable contributions every year towards the food or medical expenses of the seniors, it may be justified as a CSR spend to help support elderly, which is a permissible activity. Similarly, if advertisements with dos don'ts regarding children's nutrition are put out as part larger programme for improving health of infants and childr such spend may be justified as a CSR spend.

The spirit of the provision is against one-time, ad hc activities, or activities done purely with an eye on public relations gains—which an amendment clearly mentions as 'activities supported by the companies on sponsorship basis for deriving marketing benefits for its products or services'. (General Circular No. 14/2021, MCA).

However, the law does accept that 'brand building as a collateral benefit does not vitiate the spirit of CSR.' (ibid.).

Expenses incurred by companies for the fulfilment of any Act/ Statute of Regulations

Very often, as part of environmental clearances for projects, a spend on compensatory afforestation or on upgrading local schools or making provisions for drinking water for the community is mandated. These cannot count as CSR spend, as they are considered part of the project cost. Similarly, if compensation or skill training is mandated under land acquisition, these expenses cannot be counted towards CSR spend.

Other Exceptions

Other provisions of what do not count as CSR are very clear and need no discussion or explanations. These include:

- Activities undertaken outside India. In this regard, the new amendment has exempted 'training of Indian sports personnel representing any State or Union territory at national level or India at international level' from this condition (ibid.).

- Contribution of any amount directly or indirectly to any political party(ibid.).

Calculating CSR Spend

We already know that as per law, it has to be ensured that a 'company spends, in every financial year, at least two per cent of the average net profits of the company made during the three immediately preceding financial years' (https://mca.gov.in/).

The Ministry of Corporate Affairs has also clarified through its General Circular No. 14/2021 that even companies which have not completed three years since incorporation, but meet any one of the three criteria, fall under the purview of the law. In such cases, they need to calculate the mandatory CSR spend based on their profits once they fulfil any one of the three criteria (Ministry of Corporate Affairs, 2021).

The 'average net profit' is to be calculated in accordance with the provisions of Section 198 and exclusive of the items given under rule 2(1)(h) of the Companies (CSR Policy) Rules, 2014 (see exemptions below). As per Section 198 (5)(a), any income tax and super tax payable by the company shall not be deducted while calculating these profits. Hence, profit before tax (PBT) has to be taken into account for calculation of CSR amount. Basically, in this context, net profit means the net profit of a company as per its financial statements prepared in accordance with the applicable provisions of the Companies Act, 2013, but not including the following:

- Any profit arising from any overseas branch or branches of the company, whether operated as a separate company or otherwise, and

- Any dividend received from other companies in India, which are covered under and complying with Section 135 of the 2013 Act.

This is the amount that the company is obligated to spend as per law. As discussed before, if a company feels the need to spend more, it can certainly do so, with the necessary internal approvals. In fact, since commitments to the community on social development cannot be entirely dependent on profits, the management needs to ensure that minimum programmes do go on even in bad years when there may be no profits.

Here are a few examples of working out CSR spends:

Example 1 (Amount in Rs crore)

Details	2017–18	2018–19	2019–20
Net profit/(loss) calculated as per Section 198	147.47	203.30	102.53

Average net profit: 151.10 crore

Amount to be spent in 2020–21 (2 per cent of average net profit): 3.022 crore

Example 2 (Amount in Rs crore)

Details	2017–18	2018–19	2019–20
Net profit/(loss) as calculated as per Section 198	(-) 493.37	(-) 566.43	(-) 463.67

(-) before the figure implies negative numbers or losses

Average net profit/(loss): (-) 507.82 crore

Amount to be spent in 2020–21 (2 per cent of average net profit): Since the accumulated and therefore average profits over three years are negative, no amount needs to be spent on CSR during the year.

Example 3 (Amount in Rs crore)

Details	2017–18	2018–19	2019–20
Net profit/(loss) as calculated as per Section 198	395.35	(-) 566.43	363.68

(-) before the figure implies negative numbers or losses

Average net profit/loss: 192.60 crore

Amount to be spent in 2020–21 (2 per cent of average net profit): 3.852 crore

Working Together, Creating Synergy

The law allows different companies to come together, pool their CSR resources and carry out programmes. However, there are some stipulations. As per the law, 'A company may also collaborate with other companies for undertaking projects or programmes or CSR activities in such a manner that the CSR Committees of respective companies are in a position to report separately on such projects or programmes in accordance with these Rules' (https://mca.gov.in/content/mca/global/en/acts-rules/). It is fairly common for companies within a group, or a company and its joint venture offshoots, to come together, set up a foundation, and to pool their CSR funds into this to undertake development programmes. This allows for a larger scale and impact, and importantly, optimum utilization and sharing of overheads on a specialized unit staffed by a set of professionals who can be counted on to deliver results. Each company does not need to make its separate organizational and administrative arrangements.

The caution to be exercised however is that the CSR Committee and the Board of each company still have to formulate their own CSR policy, and approve the programmes and budgets according to the mandated spends each year. Reporting also has to be at the company level. The programmes undertaken by each company have to be distinct and identifiable. This is sometimes done by identifying different geographies for different companies, e.g., activities in states X and Y may be the responsibility of one company, those in states A, B, and C under another, etc. Alternatively, certain thematic areas or distinct activities may be allocated to different companies, e.g., all health activities across all geographies are taken up by Company A, all skill development activities by Company B, etc.

Unrelated companies too can come together to undertake CSR programmes jointly. This may happen when one company has a large foundation and is already implementing CSR initiatives, while the other does not have sufficient bandwidth for this. In such a case, the latter may choose to contribute its CSR amount to the first company's foundation, towards a specific programme. Sometimes it may happen that there is a common or shared interest. For instance, both may want to work in a specific tribal area in which one of them has already set up a field team. In such a case, the other one may support the ongoing programme.

A thematic area of activities may also be a shared interest. For instance, one company may have developed expertise in setting up and running community healthcare facilities. The second may decide that it would be more efficient for it to partner some of these than to start its own initiative. Yet another area of overlap may be the strengths emanating from the core businesses of the companies. For instance, if there is a company whose core business is engineering works, whereas the other is a manpower company, they may together set up skill development centres to train underprivileged youth in welding, turning, fitting, etc., and help to place them in entry-level jobs. This would bring the core capabilities of both the companies to play synergistically, for a meaningful social development initiative.

In such cases the responsibility of the implementing partner is high in terms of ensuring clarity of accounting, reporting, keeping track of beneficiaries, etc. It has to work with each participating company through each step of the process—from developing the proposal each year as per that company's policy and mandatory spend, ensuring implementation, monitoring, and reporting.

Credits and acknowledgements have to be appropriately assigned both with regard to physical assets as well as to activities. There should be no overlap in attributing activities or spends to more than one company, and caution must be maintained in this regard. Documentation has to be maintained such that each company can prepare its CSR reports with the required details. Moreover, complete transparency has to be maintained with all the companies concerned and the CSR Committees/Boards, about the pooled resources and partnerships. (Please also see the section on Evaluation later in this chapter, for clarification on assessment of multi-company projects.)

Coming to the question of whether CSR funds can be used to support government programmes, clarification from the Ministry of Corporate Affairs states as follows:

> The objective of CSR provisions is to involve the corporates as partners in the social development

process. Use of corporate innovations and management skills in the delivery of 'public goods' is at the core of CSR implementation by the companies. Therefore, CSR should not be interpreted as a source of financing the resource gaps in Government Schemes. However, the Board of the eligible company may undertake similar activities independently subject to fulfilment of Companies (CSR Policy) Rules, 2014 (Ministry of Corporate Affairs, 2021).

This clarifies the matter from the point of view of the corporate. However, state governments, their departments and various other wings, politicians and bureaucrats need to be educated about this, as there is effort by all of them to mobilize CSR funds for their activities. And of course, an allowable route for CSR spending is contribution to government initiatives like Swachh Bharat, Clean Ganga, etc.

CSR reporting

There are several mandatory disclosure requirements with regard to reporting CSR activities towards which companies need to ensure compliance.

Website

Every company falling in the purview of the law and having a website, is obliged to display the composition of the CSR Committee, the contents of the CSR policy, as well as the approved projects on the site.

Requirement by the Ministry of Corporate Affairs

As per the Companies Act, 2013, the directors' report needs to include a CSR annual report as per a specific format (to be found in Annexure II of Companies [Corporate Social Responsibility Policy] Amendment Rules, 2021).

The details to be reported include the following:

- Outline of the CSR policy along with details of projects to be undertaken and web link to the same;
- Composition of the CSR Committee and the meetings held during the year;
- Average net profit of the last three years;
- Prescribed CSR expenditure;
- Details of unspent amount carried over from previous years, and its use;
- Details of activities and spends separately for ongoing or multi-year projects, and projects of the current year;
- Total amount spent on each of these;
- Details of set-off across the years if any;
- Details of capital assets created;
- Impact evaluation report, if required; and
- Unspent amount, reasons for not spending, and proposed treatment.

The activity or project details that need to be reported for the ongoing year are as per the following format (with similar formats also required for ongoing projects).

(1)	(2)	(3)	(4)	(5)		(6)	(7)	(8)	(9)	(10)	(11)	
Sl. No.	Name of the project	Item from the list of activities in Schedule VII to the Act	Local Area (Yes/No)	Location of the project		Project Duration	Amount allocated for the project (in Rs)	Amount spent in the current financial year (in Rs)	Amount transferred to unspent CSR Account for the project as per Section 135(6) (in Rs)	Mode of implementation – Direct (Yes/No)	Mode of implementation – through implementing agency	
				State	District						Name	CSR Registration Number
1												
2												
3												
	TOTAL											

Source: Ministry Of Corporate Affairs Notification, 22 January, 2021.

A responsibility statement from the CSR Committee, stating that the implementation and monitoring of CSR policy are in compliance with CSR objectives and policy of the company, is also required to be given.

The recently introduced Form CSR 2 or 'Form for voluntary reporting of Corporate Social Responsibility' which can be found on the MCA site, runs into several pages (https://www.mca.gov.in/MCA21/). It is a detailed form which requires companies to provide information on CSR policy and governance, details of CSR activities, and spends for the current and previous years. It also requires the attachment of the company CSR policy, CSR report, sustainability report, as well as information on subsidiaries, etc.

It is opined that the government would be analysing the data submitted in these forms through advanced data-crunching techniques. This form will definitely add to compliance woes of the corporates as well as a fear as to how exactly the data will be used.

Related SEBI requirement

As per the new requirements brought out in May 2021 by SEBI, the top 1,000 listed companies (by market capitalization) are required to file business responsibility and sustainability reports (BRSR) annually. Other companies are encouraged to report voluntarily. This reporting is based on ESG parametres and seeks disclosures on the nine principles underlying the National Voluntary Guidelines on Responsible Business Conduct mentioned in Chapter 4. The scope of the BRSR includes but goes beyond CSR as laid down in Section 135 of the Companies Act, 2013, and captures the holistic sense of responsible business.

Ongoing Projects

Since some of the provisions related to CSR reporting refer to 'ongoing projects', it is important to understand how these are defined. As per the January 2021 notification of the Ministry of Corporate Affairs, an Ongoing Project is 'a multi-year project, stretching over more than one financial year; having a timeline not exceeding three years excluding the year of commencement; includes such project that was initially not approved as a multi-year project but whose duration has been extended beyond one year by the Board based on reasonable justification'. (General Circular No. 14, dated 22 January 2021, see MCA, 2021).

Evaluation

As per the Rules of January 2021, 'Every company having average CSR obligation of ten crore rupees or more, in the three immediately preceding financial years, shall undertake impact assessment, through an independent agency, of their CSR projects having outlays of one crore rupees or more, and which have been completed not less than one year before undertaking the impact study.' Such impact assessment needs to be carried out project-wise. The Board can decide who should carry out the assessment, and it is required to look into the report and make it part of the CSR annual report. The company is allowed to spend up to 5 per cent of that year's CSR budget or Rs 50 lakh on the evaluation, whichever is less. The Rules also permit international agencies to be contracted to undertake such evaluations.

In case two or more companies have collaborated in undertaking large projects which require impact assessment, each of them does not need to carry out an assessment separately.

They can share the evaluation report for purpose of disclosure to the respective Boards, and for inclusion as part of their CSR annual reports.

The Rule is new, and may give rise to some interpretation and confusion in the next few years. For instance, there may be lack of clarity on how 'project' is defined. Suppose, a company focuses on infrastructure development in government schools across several states. It may design each state initiative as a separate project. Hence, while no single 'project' may have an outlay of over Rs 1 crore, the total spend on this endeavour may be Rs 5 crore. Furthermore, some large CSR spends may be out of the purview of requirement—for instance, there may be a company which has a total CSR spend of Rs 4.9 crore, and may be spending all of it on a single project. However, it does not come under this mandate.

Recent reports also indicate that a social audit requirement may also be brought in for CSR initiatives, starting with Public Sector Units, and then expanding to private sector companies as well. Frameworks for the same are under preparation. What industry's reaction will be to this additional compliance requirement is yet to be seen.

While this is the legal requirement, the spirit is that significant initiatives must be formally evaluated and the feedback used to strengthen them. Boards and managements need to operate in this spirit.

Key Points in Accounting for CSR Expenses

While the CFO, the CA, and the accounts team are responsible for the accounting of CSR expenses, it would be useful for CSR managers to understand a few basics regarding this. These include:

- Where revenue expenditure is incurred on CSR, this will be accounted as an expense in the profit and loss statement of the company.
- A company can acquire/ purchase goods, and distribute/ use the same in its CSR project, e.g., purchase and distribution of sewing machines to women for their livelihoods. It is critical that expenditure is shown to have been incurred in such cases. Also, caution needs to be exercised with regard to GST in regard to goods distributed free, as some court judgments have not allowed input credits for these.
- When it comes to goods manufactured by the company and distributed free under CSR—for instance, if the company manufactures medicines and distributes these free under its CSR programme—it gets a little more difficult, and it needs to be established that this activity is not even remotely linked to the normal course of business of the company. Importantly, an expense has to be incurred. Even if the company is able to show an expense, whether the goods should be accounted for at cost price or minimum retail price is not quite clear, and at some stage, Rules may clarify the same.
- The company's CSR policy must explicitly state that any surplus arising from CSR activities shall not form a part of the business profits of the company. Such surpluses would include revenues received from CSR programmes, for example, sale of handicraft products made by beneficiaries; disposal/sale of material bought for CSR initiatives, etc. Even interest income earned by the implementing agency on funds provided under CSR comes under this head. Specific assurance has to be given in this regard. The spirit of this seems to be that the surpluses, if any, should be ploughed back into the CSR initiatives.

- CSR funds may be spent by a company for creation or acquisition of a capital asset. However, the ownership of the asset has been clarified in the 2021 Rules as follows:
  'The CSR amount may be spent by a company for creation or acquisition of a capital asset, which shall be held by –
  (a) a company established under section 8 of the Act, or a Registered Public Trust or Registered Society, having charitable objects and CSR Registration Number, or
  (b) beneficiaries of the said CSR project, in the form of self-help groups, collectives, entities; or
  (c) a public authority' (Ministry of Corporate Affairs, 22, 2021a)'.

  This means that a company cannot own any capital asset created under CSR. It has to transfer these to beneficiaries or other institutions which are public or charitable in nature. Retrospectively, with regard to assets created before 2021, these need to be transferred within six months (in special cases, nine months with Board approval). Incidentally, the expenses relating to the transfer of a capital asset may be counted as a CSR expense.
- With regard to credit for excess spending in any given year, credit can be claimed over the succeeding three years. It will lapse beyond this. This excess amount spent in any given year must be recognized as a prepaid asset in the books of accounts.
- Considerable confusion arises from the clause that the administrative expenses on CSR must not exceed 5 per cent. Fortunately, some clarifications have come in. Overheads have now been clarified as expenses 'incurred by the company for general management and administration of Corporate Social Responsibility functions in the company

but shall not include the expenses directly incurred for the designing, implementation, monitoring, and evaluation of a particular Corporate Social Responsibility project or programme' (General Circular on FAQ on CSR MCA, 2021]).

- An important point to be noted is that the 5 per cent cap applies only to the company itself. Hence, the company's foundation or implementing partners do not fall under this. NGOs and implementing partners should be fully aware of this, and discuss accordingly with corporates. Furthermore, it is left for the company to define what it will include under design, implementation, etc.

General Circular No. 14, dated 21 August 2021, clarified that salaries of staff working in the CSR department are to be counted as an administrative expense (see Ministry of Corporate Affairs, 2021). This seems to pertain to the salaries of staff managing the CSR programmes, and not those delivering it. On a practical level, it is very difficult for any entity to run a programme with 5 per cent being allowed for overheads if these salaries are included. For instance, on a spend of Rs 1 crore, the limit is Rs 5 lakh. Now if salaries of CSR staff are counted as overheads, what level of staff is being envisaged here? This is actually quite a disturbing commentary on what the government thinks should be the level and quality of people who are to be involved in CSR, and reinforces the thinking within corporates that CSR staff should be paid less than employees in other departments.

Apart from salaries, other costs mentioned in the administrative bracket are training costs of the CSR employees, utilities, office supplies, legal expenses, etc. The only relief, as mentioned, is that the salaries of those directly delivering the programmes in the field can be counted as programme implementation costs.

This clause may also be interpreted as a push not to have companies directly implement CSR, but do so through implementing partners—either their own foundations or other NGOs. Alternatively, the company has to get very creative on how it defines the various categories of expenses. Within the existing framework, several companies actually absorb many overheads (including salaries) into other departments or expense heads, claiming only 5 per cent under CSR. This seems a somewhat unfair reflection of the true cost of CSR.

- The law requires that the amount of expenditure incurred on CSR activities be disclosed by way of a note to the statement of profit and loss. As a best practice, CSR expenses should be recognized as a separate line item titled 'CSR expenditure' in the statement of profit and loss. Furthermore, the relevant note should disclose the break-up of various heads of expenses.
- Notes to CSR expenditure must contain the following details:
  (a) Gross amount required to be spent by the company during the year,
  (b) Amount approved by the Board to be spent during the year, and
  (c) Amount spent during the year on:
    - Construction/ acquisition of any asset, and
    - On purposes other than the above.

- Also, details of related party transactions, e.g., contribution to a trust/society/Section 8 company controlled by the company must be disclosed.

Key Points in the Tax Treatment of CSR Spends

When thinking of tax treatment of CSR spends, it is good to remind oneself of the fundamental reasons why the law was brought. It was that businesses should contribute to social development and inclusive growth. Another consideration—though probably not a major one—in bringing in the law was that CSR was one way of augmenting the availability of resources to meet the social development needs of the country. If tax exemptions are allowed on such spends, it amounts to the government once again subsidizing them. Hence, the basic approach is that there will be no tax exemptions allowed to CSR expenditures.

Moreover, the Finance Act, 2014, has also clarified that expenditure on CSR does not form part of business expenditure. No deductions can be claimed under Section 37 (1) of the IT Act, 1961.

There are however caveats and confusions. It is clear that in cases where a company itself takes up the execution of CSR activities directly, these CSR expenditures would be disallowed under the income tax provisions. In other words, there can be no tax benefits to a company for incurring expenditure on CSR activities which it executes. However, if the company provides funds for CSR activities to be executed through other charitable organizations such as NGOs, societies, Section 8 companies, etc., it (the company) may be able to claim tax benefits on the contributions under Section 80G, etc., of the IT Act. While this is a reading of the letter of the law, it has not been uniformly interpreted and applied, and hence it is best to seek specific professional advice in each case.

While no specific tax exemption has been extended to CSR expenditure, CSR contributions to certain institutions/

activities such as the PM Cares Fund, scientific research, rural development projects, skill development projects, agricultural extension projects, etc., which find place in Schedule VII and are already exempt under different sections of the Income Tax Act, 1961, such as Section 35(1)(ii), 35AC, etc., become eligible for tax exemption. To be eligible, these expenditures have to be incurred through specified types of organizations, for instance universities, colleges, research associations, national institutions, etc.

With regard to GST, clarity on the situation on CSR expenses is still emerging. Some claim that since CSR expenses are non-business expenses, there can be no Input Tax Credit (ITC) claims. Some court judgments seemed to veer towards the thinking that since CSR is mandated for certain class of companies, it is essential for a business to carry out these spends in order to be compliant with the law, and therefore, CSR expenses fall in the purview of 'doing or furthering business', and hence eligible for availing ITC. However, the most recent ruling [11-08-2021] by the Gujarat Authority of Advance Ruling (AAR) is that 'CSR activities, as per Companies (CSR Policy) Rules, 2014 are those activities excluded from the normal course of business of the applicant and therefore not eligible for ITC, as per Section 16(1) of the CGST Act' (gstlegal.co.in, 2021). Time will bring more clarity to this issue.

Professional advice is essential in any grey areas of IT and GST-related matters on CSR, as otherwise a company may be in breach of the law.

Actions When Mandatory CSR Spend Is Not Achieved

From time to time, companies may find it challenging to ensure complete expenditure of the mandated CSR spend.

For instance, due to field realities, activities may not proceed as planned. Or the implementing partner may have faced some challenges. It should be noted that underspending or not spending CSR amounts are being viewed increasingly seriously, and we are now in a penal regime. What started as 'Comply or Explain' is now a 'Comply or Pay' situation.

This journey started in April 2018, when it was still a 'Comply or Explain' regime. The Ministry of Corporate Affairs established the Centralized Scrutiny and Prosecution Mechanism (CSPM) for enforcement of CSR provisions on a pilot basis. Acting on its inputs, in July 2019, the Ministry issued preliminary show-cause notices to nearly 300 companies for not complying with the CSR spending requirement under the Companies Act, 2013, for the year 2015–16. In the following years too, notices were sent.

Even when companies had given a reason for not incurring the requisite spending, these were sometimes termed as 'flimsy excuses', and they were held in default of the provisions of Section 135 read with Section 134 (3) of the Act. The notices made it clear that the defaulting companies would be punishable with fines which would 'not be less than fifty thousand rupees but which may extend to twenty-five lakh rupees, and every officer of the company who was in default would be punishable with imprisonment for a term which could extend to three years, or with both'.

The notices asked such companies to either transfer the requisite unspent CSR amount to any of the Funds listed under Schedule VII or spend the unspent amount as per its CSR policy in any subjects or areas mentioned under Schedule VII of the Act. The notices however assured the companies that on evidence of document(s) for the spending of the unspent CSR amount, there would be no prosecution against the company and its identified officer-in-default.

Changes to the Companies Act brought about in September 2019 swung to a drastic position of writing these penalties into law with fines as well as imprisonment of the officers concerned for transgressions. Fortunately, the January 2021 amendments rolled back the clauses with regard to imprisonment. But transgressions are still a civil offence, and there are still serious consequences for non-compliance, as discussed below.

Hence it is critical for CSR managers within companies to rigorously monitor the expenses to ensure that there is no crisis of underspending at the last minute. During the course of the year, the CSR Committee and the Board must be kept informed of any anticipated challenges, as ultimately they are responsible. They may provide guidance on how the challenges can be overcome, what the alternatives could be, approve changes in plans, etc.

It may be noted that it is not enough for a company to transfer its money to an implementing partner—that does not count as a spend. The money has to be actually spent on the proposed activities. It has been clarified by the Ministry of Corporate Affairs that 'Mere disbursal of funds for implementation of a project does not amount to spending unless the implementing agency utilizes the whole amount' (Ministry of Corporate Affairs, 2021). Else, it is deemed unspent by the company, and needs to be handled as per the provisions discussed below. There is likely to be some confusion in this regard in the future on whether the implementing partners have to transfer back the unspent money on 31 March to the company. Some opine that it may not be necessary, though the safe thing to do as per a reading of the FAQs of the MCA is to do so. Only time will clarify this.

However, if despite all due diligence, underspending occurs, the CSR Committee and the Board need to be given adequate and convincing reasons and explanations. As per Section 7.0 of the General Circular on FAQs on CSR (see Ministry of Corporate Affairs, 2021), unspent amounts with regard to ongoing projects will need to be transferred to a separate bank account of the company called 'Unspent CSR Account', within thirty days of the end of the financial year.

Except for the case of ongoing projects, where amount unspent at the year-end is carried over, in all other cases the unspent amount has to be transferred to any Fund included in Schedule VII of the Act, viz., (a) Swachh Bharat Kosh (b) Clean Ganga Fund (c) PMNRF (d) PM CARES Fund and (e) any other fund set up by the Central government and notified by the Ministry of Corporate Affairs for socio-economic development and relief and welfare of the Scheduled Castes, Scheduled Tribes, other backward classes, minorities, and women, within six months from the end of the financial year.

The reasons for underspending as well as the plans for the utilization of the amount have to be recorded in the directors' report, and also reported in the website of the Ministry of Corporate Affairs. Needless to say, when an unspent amount is carried forward, this CSR spend is over and above the mandatory CSR spend for the next year. A company may have underspent on more than one project in a given year. It does not need to open different accounts for each of these unspent amounts. All unspent funds pertaining to ongoing projects of a given financial year can be pooled into the company's 'Unspent CSR Account'. However, if it once again has unspent funds in the next financial year, it does need to open a separate account for that year.

It seems that a special National Unspent CSR Fund is on the anvil, and once that is created, it is likely that such unspent funds will have to be transferred there.

Boards, CSR Committees, and managements need to note that the latest amendments of September 2020 state that

> If a company is in default in complying with the provisions of sub-section (5) or sub-section (6), the company shall be liable to a penalty of twice the amount required to be transferred by the company to the Fund specified in Schedule VII or the Unspent Corporate Social Responsibility Account, as the case may be, or one crore rupees, whichever is less, and every officer of the company who is in default shall be liable to a penalty of one-tenth of the amount required to be transferred by the company to such Fund specified in Schedule VII, or the Unspent Corporate Social Responsibility Account, as the case may be, or two lakh rupees, whichever is less.
>
> https://www.mca.gov.in/Ministry/pdf/AmendmentAct_29092020.pdf

The non-transference of the unspent CSR amount within the required time frame carries penal consequences as described above. Moreover, non-compliance with other aspects of the law, e.g., not disclosing the unspent amount in the CSR annual report, also carries consequences.

The scrutiny of CSR spends is intense at all levels. The Parliamentary Committee on Finance has recently expressed concern over the monitoring of these spends and has asked for more stringent measures in this direction (*Economic Times*, 28 March 2022).

All in all, safety lies in ensuring that the required CSR amount is spent within the year, unless there are very strong reasons why it cannot be done. The Board, the CSR Committee, as well as the top management will be extremely uneasy if this does not happen, as the company is bound to come under scrutiny for this, and possibly face harsh consequences. The only exception is when projects are designed and approved as ongoing multi-year projects.

6
Operationalizing CSR: Some Practical Aspects

The first step in the CSR journey of a corporate is the formulation of a CSR policy. This is not only a legal requirement but also a statement of the intent, philosophy, approach, and scope of a corporate's CSR. While the law requires that the CSR policy has certain elements, in reality it needs to go much beyond.

The CSR Policy as per the Law

The Companies Act, 2013, requires that the CSR Committee shall 'formulate and recommend to the Board, a Corporate Social Responsibility Policy which shall indicate the activities to be undertaken by the company as specified in Schedule VII' (and when there is no requirement for a CSR committee, the Board will take this duty upon itself).

As per the requirement, the CSR policy is defined by the MCA as follows:

> "CSR Policy" means a statement containing the approach and direction given by the Board of a company, taking into account the recommendations of its CSR Committee, and includes guiding principles for selection, implementation and monitoring of activities as well as formulation of the annual action plan.
>
> MCA Notification, 22 January 2021

While it is important that a company's CSR policy should comply with the requirements of the law, it is equally important to understand that a policy is a fundamental document for an organization—a company's statement of intent and reflective of the philosophy. Hence it needs to go beyond the points mentioned.

Like any other good policy, it must be a guide to thinking, decision making, and action. It should provide broad guidelines while allowing scope for flexibility in implementation. Care needs to be taken to make it simple and clear, specific, uniform, appropriate to the company, and comprehensive. Of course, it also needs to cover all the relevant points to be compliant to the law.

The process of development of the CSR policy is also important. While the process may be driven by the CSR team, it needs the involvement of key internal stakeholders—from operations to HR to finance. The participation of senior management as well as key members of the Board/CSR Committee at some points of the process will ensure strategic alignment between business and CSR. External experts from the fields of CSR and social development, as well as relevant subject matter experts, could help to generate new perspectives and validate the policy. Inputs of key external stakeholders, whoever they may be for the company, may help to make it more material, grounded, and acceptable.

A good CSR policy in the Indian context could include the following sections:

- Title
- Applicability and validity
- CSR vision/mission
- CSR focus areas (mapped to Schedule VII of the Companies Act, 2013)
- Priority geographical areas
- CSR governance and management structures
- Implementation mechanisms and structures
- Implementation details
- Details of projects and ongoing projects
- Budgeting, treatment of previous excess spends and of underspends
- Treatment of surpluses
- Monitoring and reporting protocols
- Protocols for measurement of outcomes and impacts, and evaluation
- Organization structure and responsibilities
- Plans and budgets for the year

In order to help those setting out on this journey, Annexure 1 gives a sample CSR policy. It does not refer to any specific company but combines good points from several policies.

Deciding on the Menu of CSR Activities

Schedule VII, which specifies what thrust areas of activities are permissible under the law, is very wide and as mentioned, most socio-economic development activities can be fitted into the framework. So while the Schedule must be kept in mind to define the boundaries, it does not help to narrow the field! The Schedule, when read in conjunction with the points in the section titled 'Activities not Counted as CSR as per the Law', can help to rule out certain activities.

But narrowing down on what to do is a difficult task, especially if the company does not have a tradition of involvement in social causes. In deciding the scope of activities, there is an interplay of factors from the organization's core values to its history, to its understanding of CSR, to the nature of its business, its impact on the environment and community, its location, to its stakeholders and their perceptions, to what the needs analysis throws up. (Chapter 7 discusses some tools like needs assessment, stakeholder analysis, materiality mapping, etc., which can help focus the priorities and develop the CSR strategy, plan, and budget.)

It has been seen that in family-owned businesses, it is sometimes the vision and passion of the founder which govern the direction of CSR. For instance, if a founder or someone in the family is passionate about heritage, the company CSR may veer towards related activities. If another believes that senior citizens are vulnerable and need support, then programmes are likely to have that bent.

The nature of the business operations has significant influence on the shape of its CSR. For instance, IT and software companies tend to move into the education space, probably because they believe that improving education is necessary for a future pipeline of employees, and also because their own operations are a natural fit. A software company taking up a large-scale push for teaching coding to government school children finds this a fit with its operations and skills. Such an initiative helps them contribute in a space which they understand well and where they can make a difference.

That said, it helps if a corporate draws feedback from a cross section of its stakeholders, formally or informally, on what its CSR thrust should focus on. This focus on materiality helps in aligning the CSR initiatives better.

The law does not say anything about how many thrust areas of activities a company may take up. It may choose to focus on one area in Schedule VII, or spread its activities and budgets across any number of them. Also, there is nothing in the law which stops a company from adding or dropping activities in any thrust area from year to year—as long as their policy is wide enough. Of course, the law does want that programmes should not be ad hoc but that they should build up towards impact, which is possible only with sustained activities. Hence, from an outcomes perspective, it makes sense to focus on a few thrust areas and build on initiatives over a period of time, so that there is significant impact.

After deciding the broad thrust of activities, it is important to decide on the specific initiatives. For instance, if a company decides that education would be the basic thrust, there are still myriad decisions which must be taken. To highlight just a few:

- Which level: Early childhood education? Primary education? Higher education?

- To support government schools? Or start one's own subsidized school? Or support individual children with scholarships?
- To focus on infrastructure, or teacher training, or para-teachers, or tuitions for children?

So it is not simple! Hence, when the CSR policy and strategy are being made for the first time, detailed discussion is important. And since nothing is static, it may be useful to repeat the exercise periodically.

Box 6.1: Catch Them Young

Corporate Award for Excellence in CSR: CSR Spend Below Rs 1 crore

Paranjape Autocast's flagship CSR project on Early Childhood Education was the winner of the Corporate Award for Excellence in CSR in its category for its work with fifty-two Anganwadi centres of Khandala taluka in Satara district. The initiative touches the lives of over a thousand children in the age group of three to six. The effort is to strengthen child-centric and activity-based learning in these centres through training and ongoing capacity building of Anganwadi workers and helpers. Apart from training, the Anganwadis are provided teaching–learning material. Regular monitoring and mentoring of the Anganwadi workers helps to sustain the momentum. The parents and community are made active participants in the process.

Based on: http://www.paranjapeautocast.com/csr.html

A very positive change that has recently been brought about by the government is that as per the new rules, CSR projects can be designed as longer-duration interventions or ongoing projects. As per the rules, an '"Ongoing Project" means a multi-year project undertaken by a Company in fulfilment of its CSR obligation having timelines not exceeding three years excluding the financial year in which it was commenced' (General Circular No. 14/2021, MCA). Commencement means that some work order or contract pertaining to the planned activity has been issued. This will help to design more stable programmes with a longer vision.

The rules also allow the Board to convert an activity designed as a single-year activity into an ongoing activity, provided the Board is convinced there is reasonable justification to do this.

The shape of the implementable programme will depend on the needs assessment and the community situation, and priorities need to be drawn up based on detailed discussions. The plan and budget need to be built ground-up, based on these considerations.

A question that comes up is that if a corporate is working on several thrust areas, how does it decide how much to spend on each. In other words, how much of what? Few organizations would start out with a set formula like: 'We will spend 45 per cent on education and skills; 25 per cent on health; 25 per cent on women empowerment; the remaining 5 per cent is towards admin.' Such precise demarcation is impractical. However, it is useful to do an analysis of the spends and categorize them on the basis of thrust area, and examine from year to year whether the trend remains the same, or whether it is changing, and why. So the thrust-area-wise allocation of resources is usually not an ab-initio decision, but useful for post-facto analysis.

Deciding the Geography of CSR

The stipulation as to where a company should undertake its CSR activities is one of the confusing aspects of the provisions, and an area where the wisdom of the CSR Committee and the Board comes into play. Section 135 states that 'the company shall give preference to the local area and areas around it where it operates'. The underlying logic could be that it draws resources from its local environment, and also any negative impacts are typically on the local environment. This is true in the case of say manufacturing units, power plants, mining, etc. However, it is not necessarily true in the same sense for a software company or a retail chain. Moreover, how is 'local area' to be interpreted when the head office is in one city and the company has operations dispersed across many cities? What about an airline that flies across the country? Or a company which builds highways that cover hundreds of kilometres? Or a telecom company which puts up its towers all over?

On another dimension, there has been concern that most CSR spending is taking place in a few metros and a few states, and is not benefitting really under-served and remote areas. To elaborate on this point, as per government data, in the first six years since the law has come into force, over 25 per cent of CSR spending has been in the three states of Maharashtra, Karnataka and Tamil Nadu, whereas the states of Arunachal Pradesh, Manipur, Meghalaya, Nagaland, Tripura, and Sikkim put together saw a little under 2.5 per cent CSR funds coming their way. Of course, this can also be seen in the light of state sizes and populations, but even apart from these, such disparities are inevitable if companies have to spend in their local areas. The under-served and remote areas do not have industries with mandatory CSR spends!

Fortunately, the Ministry in its latest amended FAQs gives some clarity on this matter. Recognizing that some activities transcend narrow geographic boundaries, and that the advent of IT has also made these boundaries obsolete, the Ministry has stated that:

> The spirit of the Act is to ensure that CSR initiatives are aligned with the national priorities and enhance engagement of the corporate sector towards achieving Sustainable Development Goals (SDGs). Thus, the preference to local area in the Act is only directory and not mandatory in nature and companies need to balance local area preference with national priorities (General Circular No. 14/2021, MCA).

Table 6.1: States and CSR spends, 2014–2020

Six-year Cumulative CSR Spend	States and UTs
Less than Rs 100 crore	Andaman and Nicobar, Arunachal, Chandigarh, Daman and Diu, Dadra and Nagar Haveli, Lakshadweep, Mizoram, Nagaland, Puducherry, Sikkim
Rs 100–1,000 crore	Bihar, Chhattisgarh, Goa, Himachal Pradesh, erstwhile state of Jammu and Kashmir*, Jharkhand, Manipur, Meghalaya, Punjab
Rs 1,000–5,000 crore	Andhra Pradesh, Assam, Delhi, Gujarat, Haryana, Kerala, Madhya Pradesh, Rajasthan, Tamil nadu, Telangana, West Bengal

Six-year Cumulative CSR Spend	States and UTs
Rs 5,000–10,000 crore	Karnataka
Over Rs 10,000 crore	Maharashtra

Source: Based on data from www.csr.gov.in

*The state of J&K was reorganized into two Union Territories—Jammu and Kashmir and Ladakh with effect from 31 October 2019.

The vision of the Boards comes into play with regard to the geography of CSR, in interpreting this requirement, and specially the phrase 'give preference to'.

Infrastructure, manufacturing, and resource companies tend to work in geographies around their operations. This is probably because their businesses have a direct and usually detrimental effect on the environment and the community in the vicinity. Land may have been acquired for such projects, which affects the livelihoods of the communities, and often as a response, skill training or livelihood projects are taken up in the local community. In case of manufacturing or resource extraction, there may be depletion of water resources or impacts on water quality, in which case the company may take up watershed programmes, lake restoration, etc. Social licence to operate and widespread support from the local community are very critical for such companies, and due to this, they may also take up generic community development activities—from working with government schools to putting up primary health facilities. These activities meet the felt needs and touch the lives of most of the community.

Different companies have different approaches to the issue of geography. For example, some are still going strictly by the letter of the law and spending 100 per cent in the location of their operations. Others have struck a formula for dividing the amount between the head office and factories or plants. Yet others spend about half around the area of their operations and the remaining in remote or under-served areas which may have nothing to do with their business. Yet others are contributing to national-level programmes.

There can be justification for any of these. After all, one cannot say there are not many pockets of great need in the best of our metros. Moreover, if a company in Bengaluru chooses to spend there, it can monitor the programmes better, leverage its employees for volunteering, and also improve the visibility of the spend to key stakeholders. All of which are justifiable objectives. Similarly there can be justification to spend away from the area of operations. As mentioned, remote and inaccessible areas, tribal communities, etc., do need special support and CSR resources can help.

Box 6.2: CRISIL Foundation—Financial Inclusion in the North-east

National CSR Award for contributing to: 'CSR in Challenging Circumstances, North East'

CRISIL Foundation's 'Mein Pragati' project in Assam 'aims to empower socially and economically disadvantaged sections of society by strengthening their financial capabilities'. Launched in 2015, Mein Pragati started with the goal to empower one lakh rural women, with the help of Rashtriya Gramin Vikas Nidhi as implementation partner.

Starting with financial awareness, the project has gone on to tackle the challenges of achieving long-term behaviour change. This is done through community volunteers who help to tackle last-mile constraints and sustain change. These volunteers are trained and certified through online platforms. They have facilitated financial connectivity to over a lakh people across 400-plus villages, through access to various government welfare schemes. The volunteers charge a small fee for the services they provide, thus making the initiative sustainable.

Based on: https://www.crisil.com/en/home/newsroom/press-releases/2019/10/crisil-foundation-bags-national-csr-award.

A factor that must be kept in mind is that CSR programmes need time to deliver impacts. When there is a boundary of 'the local area', it is likely that initiatives will build up year-on-year and the benefits will be sustainable. If the local area condition is not applied, there is a chance that a company may take up programmes in different areas from year to year.

Moreover when there are no geographical limits, there may be pressure on companies from different stakeholders to undertake ad hoc activities without a sound logic, in places where they do not have implementation strength. It is not unknown for companies to be asked by people in power to undertake CSR programmes in their areas of interest, such as in constituencies, home towns, etc., even when these are far removed from the company's operations, and any link between the company and the suggested geography is difficult to find. There are also many examples of companies taking up visible CSR projects in areas which are of interest to important stakeholders to win favourable attention. And it is also not unknown for companies to reduce the activity once the person for whom the programme was being done is no longer in power!

State governments too may indicate their preference for specific areas or contribution into their programmes. Having a policy which clearly states *where* the company will take up CSR can help to some extent to subvert these pressures. The important point is that whatever the decision, it needs to be taken with adequate thought, justification, and consistency, and with a long-term view. Both the criticality of the needs of the community and the strategic requirements of the business have to be kept in mind.

As of now, the government has not questioned the decision of Boards on where they have spent/plan to spend their CSR funds, and it has allowed them to interpret this clause. Hence companies and Boards should use this discretion to do what they believe to be right and fitting with regard to their vision.

The government has however mandated that CPSEs should spend a significant part of their CSR funds in aspirational districts. While as yet there is no explicit directive for private sector CSR with regard to these aspirational districts, there may at some stage be an active encouragement of this.

Deciding on an Implementation Strategy

As per the currently prevalent rules, the Board of a company may decide how its CSR activities will be undertaken, viz., through:

- the company itself,
- a registered public trust,
- a registered society,

- a company established under Section 8 of the Companies Act, 2013, or
- or any entity established under an Act of Parliament or a state legislature.

The registered trust, society, or Section 8 company mentioned above may be set up by the company by itself, or along with other companies, or by its holding or subsidiary or associate company, or it could be one established by the Central government or a state government.

Companies may also implement through a trust, society or Section 8 company not set up by the company or its associates, or the government. In such cases, it must be ensured that the implementing agency or partner has an established track record of three years in undertaking similar programmes. It should also be ensured that the company has specified the project or progammes to be undertaken through these entities, the modalities of utilization of funds on such projects and programmes, and the monitoring and reporting mechanisms.

As discussed earlier, the rules also allow for a company to collaborate with other companies to undertake its CSR initiatives, with the proviso that it must be possible for the CSR Committee of each company to report separately with regard to its own CSR.

As per the new rules, any CSR implementing agency (apart from a company implementing its own CSR), has to register itself with the Ministry of Corporate Affairs, using CSR Form 1. This applies to all entities—NGOs, trusts, company foundations, etc. Without this registration, no organization can implement CSR activities.

It may also be noted that it is not essential that the company follows only one route for implementation, subject to the condition that its policy allows for this and the due approvals are taken in the annual plan. It may, for instance, choose to do some activities itself, and some others through its foundation or other NGO partners.

So basically, a company can decide to undertake CSR directly, through an in-house team; or it can set up a foundation for this, and get them to implement on its behalf; or it can get unrelated NGOs to implement on its behalf. How will it decide which of these it will choose as the major vehicle for its CSR? The decision is a typical business 'make or buy' decision. Senior management, CSR Committee and the Board may have to take several factors into consideration in making this call, including:

- Does the company have the bandwidth and professional capability to manage CSR?
- Does it have or does it want to set up a separate entity and manage it?
- What is its CSR vision, and which mechanism will meet this vision better—to do it itself, through an in-house foundation, or outsourcing it to unrelated specialized agencies?
- Through which mode are the initiatives likely to be more impactful?
- Which will be the more efficient option?
- What are the risks involved in each option, and which is best from this perspective?
- Will it be possible to ensure alignment of objectives when working with outside agencies?
- Through which mode can integration of environmental and social objectives into the business agenda be better achieved?
- Which mode offers better opportunities for employee involvement?

- Will the company get the due positive collateral with key stakeholders if it works with outside agencies?
- How will it ensure credibility, transparency, accountability, delivery, reporting, etc., when working with an outside agency?

These and other questions have to be considered carefully before taking a decision. As mentioned, it is not an either/or strategy. Companies often use a combination of means—carrying out some activities directly, some through their own CSR arms, and some specialized functions (e.g., providing medical services) through contracting with outside agencies.

Increasingly, large companies or groups with substantial spends are setting up their own foundations, often structured as Section 8 companies (Incidentally, the term 'foundation' has no legal meaning. 'Foundation' is often the word used to indicate the social, non-profit nature of an organization). While the overheads of this option may seem higher, companies see many advantages to this when compared to working with unrelated outside agencies—starting from integration and alignment of social and environmental goals with overall business objectives, to greater accountability, to having strong brand recognition, and halo effect from corporate to foundation and vice versa.

Each company needs to weigh the questions and make its choice. There is no one right way. However, working with the spirit that collaborations and partnerships of different kinds are all enriching—corporate–corporate, corporate–NGO, corporate–government—is a useful mantra.

There are several new types of partnership possibilities opening up—with technology providers, with social enterprises, with agencies offering specialized products and services. Many of these are innovative and can help bring in new solutions or efficiencies. It is important for CSR managers to be aware and connected with these developments.

Role of International Agencies

The new amendments have allowed space for international agencies in CSR, but for limited purpose. The clause says: 'A company may engage international organizations for designing, monitoring and evaluation of the CSR projects or programmes as per its CSR policy as well as for capacity building of their own personnel for CSR.' In other words, though international agencies may be brought in for specific specialized activities, they cannot take up implementation of CSR programmes. Furthermore, it is not immediately apparent what the definition of an international agency is. If a company desires to use the services of such agencies, it needs to provide for the same in its CSR policy.

Organizational Arrangements for CSR

For many reasons, corporates may see setting up their own foundations as the most effective and reliable way to carry out their CSR. Many of these entities are structured as Section 8 (not-for-profit) companies, which is a form of institution that corporates are familiar and comfortable with. Since Section 8 companies have a higher level of governance and transparency requirements as compared to trusts and societies, this is a good direction.

Sometimes, rather than setting up a separate entity, the CSR function may be looked after by an in-house team. Such a team might be constituted as a separate CSR department. Alternatively, the CSR team may be part of some other department—human resources, public relations, corporate communications, strategy, etc. The placement of the CSR team within a department signals both the conceptualization of the purpose and function of CSR, as well as the approach and activities it will take up, and signals the significance the management wishes to portray for its CSR activities. In some cases, CSR teams may have matrix reporting—to the business head and to the CSR head. As in all matrix relationships, these have to be managed with care!

Some corporates are taking a more holistic view. While they have foundations to implement their CSR programmes, the head of the foundation also has a seat at the top business table. This is usually done by designating the person as 'president, sustainability' in the business entity, as well as CEO or head of the foundation. This may be the way going forward, if social and environmental concerns have to be integrated into the core concerns of the business in the quest for sustainability.

With all these implications, it would be important to take decisions on organization design after adequate internal brainstorming on what CSR means to the company, before doing the hard-wiring in terms of organization structure.

Depending on the size, scale, approach, and aspirations, the size of the CSR team varies. If a company implements its own CSR, it may have a large team, from head of department to field staff, deployed across various geographies of operations. On the other hand, if it is a coordination function, where activities are carried out through NGOs or other implementing agencies, it may be a small team which is basically tasked with the responsibility of carrying out due diligence for selection of implementing agencies; the preparation of clear memoranda of understanding or contracts and agreements for implementation of activities; and monitoring, evaluation, and reporting.

Again, it is up to the management of each company to weigh the organizational requirement and accordingly design the function.

Some of the advantages of setting up a separate foundation are mentioned below. Many of these are relevant in the two common debates, viz., when the company is deciding whether it should set up a separate foundation, or implement CSR through an internal CSR department; and when it is trying to decide whether it should work with an external implementing agency or set up its own foundation. Many companies see the advantages of setting up an in-house foundation as follows:

- Specialized people with expertise and skills to carry out the whole cycle of CSR and effectively deliver the outcomes;
- A body that is aware of the nuances of the legal requirements and has the support of the corporate to set up required systems and processes to meet these requirements;
- An independent team which is able to keep business imperatives in context, without diluting social objectives;
- Ease of transfer of funds from the corporate to the foundation, because Boards, CSR Committees, etc., will more easily trust its credibility;
- Good branding—even though the company's foundation may be a separate entity, the relationship to the business entity is quite clear, thus reflecting good work done by the entity directly on the business;
- Easier communications internally and externally when the entity is related to the business;
- The ability to serve a group of companies and provide synergies;
- The ability to work with other companies to implement their CSR and also leverage government and other resources; and

- Last but not the least, since a foundation is an institution in its own right, the possibility for legacy creation, and for development activities to continue to function irrespective of business imperatives.

Even when a company has its own foundation, it is still useful to work on certain initiatives with external NGOs which usually have much more specialized expertise, deep presence, and a long history of community engagement. Moreover, this helps bring in a more objective perspective on the CSR programmes.

7
The Responsibilities

CSR: A Responsibility at the Highest Level of Governance

The ultimate responsibility for CSR has been given by the law to the company's Board and its subcommittee, the CSR Committee. It is they who are to ensure the compliance of the company's CSR in letter and spirit.

The Board needs to ensure appointment of the CSR Committee as and when the company requires one. It needs to ensure nominating the appropriate persons to the CSR Committee and also see to it that the Committee meets with the criterion of having an independent director, where applicable. Probably, the most important responsibility for the Board and the CSR Committee is at the beginning of the company's CSR journey—in the development of a CSR policy. It is this which creates the framework for the organization's CSR for years to come, and also integrates social and environmental concerns with the business agenda.

The CSR Committee needs to spend adequate time in discussing the why, what, where, and how of the company's CSR. It needs to ensure that there is an overarching mission/vision for the CSR, over and above routine operations. It needs to push for the policy to have a stakeholder focus, and also for the evangelization of the policy within the organization for the creation of an overall corporate culture. Similarly, the Board needs to spend adequate time on CSR in the first few meetings. The Board and the CSR Committee need to ensure a long-term programmatic vision, which ensures commitment beyond the mandatory CSR spend for the year.

They must also clarify the role they visualize for the company's CSR. There can be several roles that CSR initiatives could play, but the choice must be consciously made. Is the objective to create a difference locally? Is the aim to create replicable models? Is it to provide last-mile connectivity for delivery of government programmes? Is it about strengthening and capacity building systems? Is it about reforming systems?

They must constantly push the company to ensure that the CSR efforts

- Are focused on making a difference;
- Are designed with a clear focus on outcomes and impacts;
- Are strategic;
- Have a clear focus on sustainability and scalability;
- Keep the SDGs, larger national goals, and missions as the context;
- Are delivered efficiently and are based on strong systems, processes, and best practices;
- Are evaluated as required.

Profits and mandatory CSR spend calculations will of course vary from year to year, but social development initiatives are long-term by their very nature, and commitments made to the community cannot go up and down with the profits. Boards own the responsibility to ensure that these initiatives are ongoing, and not on-and-off affairs.

Moreover, a policy cannot be a static document. Hence, the CSR Committee may like to call for a review and discussion of the policy at appropriate intervals, to ensure that it is responsive to emerging needs and conditions.

From year to year it is up to the CSR Committee (or the Board, if there is no CSR Committee) to closely scrutinize the proposed programmes for adherence to Schedule VII and to ensure that they are in line with the law and approved policy; that they are impactful initiatives; that all necessary details of the proposal are in place, e.g., where the activities are to be implemented, who is to implement, what is the mandatory spend for the year as per the profit calculations, and whether the CSR administrative spend is contained within 5 per cent of the mandatory spend. They need to review the progress of the activities on a regular basis, and ensure completion of activities and spend, especially where these are multi-year initiatives. They need to focus the attention of the CSR teams and the management on outcomes and impacts, and their assessment.

After careful consideration of all this, the CSR Committee needs to make its recommendations to the Board, which will discuss and approve this. With this, they become responsible for the CSR of the company. At the end of the year, the CSR Committee chair has to co-sign the CSR annual report.

When a company underspends on its CSR requirements for the year, the role of the Committee and the Board is very much in focus. They need to reassure themselves not only about the genuineness of the reasons for the underspending but also to ensure that the necessary provisions are made for carrying over the amount (in case of ongoing projects), or its donation to allowable organizations (in case it was unspent in projects which are not ongoing) through proper mechanisms. The underspend and the reasons thereof, as well as the assurances that unspent amount will be treated as per legal requirements, need to be explicitly and transparently stated in the Board's report and other necessary filings.

The Board also needs to review the CSR policy from time to time and make necessary changes. The Board needs to assure itself that the CSR policy, composition of the CSR Committee, and annual reports are compliant with the law and are disclosed on the company website as per law.

Impact assessment for certain categories of CSR projects is now mandatory. The Board needs to ensure these are carried out, and to review and report the findings. Even when it is not mandatory, it may encourage evaluations of the company's major initiatives from time to time. As a good practice, CSR Committee and Board members may occasionally physically visit or participate in CSR activities to get a flavour of the ground-level functioning. Their involvement and guidance can help CSR teams to make programmes more strategic, impactful, and efficient.

As the top governance bodies, the Board and the CSR Committee need to ensure compliance and adherence to the company CSR policy. However, even more critically, they need to remind the company that merely complying with the law, viz., Section 135 of the Companies Act, 2013, is only one part of being socially responsible. It is up to the Board and the CSR Committee to push for the company to integrate the spirit of CSR, i.e., moving from a shareholder perspective to a stakeholder perspective, and integrating the larger principles of good governance.

The Board with its 360° vision of the company's functioning can drive integration of stakeholder concerns into the company's core functioning, towards minimizing the company's negative impacts on the environment, community and society, and maximizing the positive impacts.

Box 7.1 : One Group, Three Awards

The Mahindra Group was the only corporate to be honoured with National CSR Awards for contribution across three National Priority Area categories:

1. Overall Excellence in CSR
2. Education: Project Nanhi Kali
3. Agriculture and Rural Development: Integrated Watershed Management Programme

This is definitely indicative of the commitment at each level of the organization.

Project Nanhi Kali: Launched in 1996 by the K.C. Mahindra Education Trust, with the aim of educating underprivileged girls in India, Nanhi Kali focuses on enabling underprivileged girls to complete ten years of schooling. The project provides daily academic support, access to an adaptive learning software via digital tablets, sports curriculum, as well as an annual school supplies kit, which allow the girls to attend school with dignity. It has supported over 4.5 lakh girls since inception (for more see https://www.nanhikali.org/).

Integrated Watershed Management Programme: This PPP initiative of Mahindra and Mahindra in partnership with the Goverment of Madhya Pradesh, aims to increase the groundwater table of the region. Through this, agricultural productivity has been enhanced, and standard of living of people of about forty villages positively impacted.

Key components of the project include construction of check dams, ponds, tanks, bunds, as well as soil and water conservation structures. Plantation of tree cover is another vital activity. The project has touched the lives of tens of thousands of people, and all aspects have been undertaken with active community participation through local Village-Level Water Committees and Self-Help Groups.

Based on: https://csrbox.org/India_CSR_Project_Mahindra-&-Mahindra-Ltd-Integrated-Watershed-Management-Program-Madhya-Pradesh

CSR Responsibilities of Senior Management

The CEO or MD carry the ultimate responsibility, and in this role, have to co-sign the company's CSR annual report with the chair of the CSR Committee. Hence, the CEO, along with the chair of the CSR Committee, shoulder the responsibility for the company's CSR. The chief financial officer (CFO) or any the person responsible for financial management of the company has a critical responsibility. This functionary needs to certify to the effect that the CSR funds disbursed by the company have been utilized for the purposes and in the manner as approved by the Board. Serious consequences for non-compliance have been laid down for 'every officer in default'. As per the amended rules:

> If a company is in default in complying with the provisions of sub-section (5) or sub-section (6), the company shall be liable to a penalty of twice the amount required to be transferred by the company to the Fund specified in Schedule VII or the Unspent Corporate Social Responsibility Account, as the case may be, or one crore rupees, whichever is less, and every officer of the company who is in default shall be liable to a penalty of one-tenth of the amount required to be transferred by the company to such Fund specified in Schedule VII, or the Unspent Corporate Social Responsibility Account, as the case may be, or two lakh rupees, whichever is less (The Companies [Amendment] Act, 2020).

This replaces the original benign injunction in the 2013 Act that 'if the company fails to spend such amount, the Board shall, in its report made under clause (o) of sub-section (3) of section 134, specify the reasons for not spending the amount'.

The law has not quite specified which officers will be considered to be in default in this regard. As in everything else however, the ultimate responsibility for all actions of a company is the CEO's. Hence she/he has to ensure that the company meets its CSR obligations in letter and spirit. It seems the CFO may also be counted among those responsible, as maybe the CSR head.

With regard to CSR, the CEO's responsibilities would also include ensuring that there is a proper organization structure with clear responsibilities for CSR activities; a proper planning process taking into account strategic business needs, stakeholder involvement, clear operational procedures and deliverables; and reviews and evaluation of the same. Of course the CEO needs to ensure timely resourcing for the CSR team to carry out the plan; and facilitation of processes of the CSR Committee and the Board.

As a function, CSR is not always taken as a serious, critical, and professional activity of the corporate. Therefore it is for the CEO to support the CSR mission by being seen to be invested and involved in it, communicating its importance and its centrality to the business. Only a CEO can raise the status of CSR within the organization so that it is taken seriously internally. Also, CSR heads need to be made part of core business discussions, just as other heads of departments are.

The CEO also needs to create an environment conducive for employee volunteering. Even though this is not legally required, it does bring benefits to the people function, and creates a culture of community and environmental responsibility. The role of the HR function is critical in supporting this. As importantly, the CEO needs to speak about the company's CSR in external forums also, presenting it genuinely as part of the core activities.

In good years, there is money to spend on CSR. But in bad years, when there is little or no mandatory spend, the CEO has to ensure outlay of adequate resources so that the bare minimum activities continue, and there is no break in essential services to the communities. Driving this mindset, the provision of necessary resources and getting required approvals from the Board are key responsibilities of the CEO.

Beyond the requirements of India's legal mandate, a good CEO takes the lead towards integrating community and environmental concerns into core business functions, and to meet the spirit of frameworks like UNGC, Sustainability Reporting, ESG rating, etc.

The company secretary too has many responsibilities relating to CSR. These include ensuring:

- The constitution of a CSR Committee as per law;
- Regular and timely meetings of the Committee as required (twice a year) and placing the recommendations to the Board for approval;
- The formulation of a CSR policy by the CSR Committee and approval of the same by the Board which will directly undertake this job if the company is not required to have a CSR Committee;
- That the calculation of the mandatory spend for the year, based on profits for the last three years, is correct;
- That the activity plans are as per the law (e.g., compliance to Schedule VII, expenditure as per calculation, mode of implementation, geographic location, limit on administrative expenditure, etc.), and the presentation of the same in requisite detail for discussion and recommendation by the CSR Committee or Board, and placing the same for approval to the Board;
- Reporting progress to the CSR Committee and the Board;
- Placing required information on the website (e.g., composition of the CSR Committee, CSR policy, etc.);
- Reporting to the Ministry of Corporate Affairs through CSR Form 2;
- Reporting to SEBI as part of responsible business reporting;
- Presenting required CSR details in the annual report as part of the Directors' Report as per requirement, including explanation for underspend if any;
- The requisite approvals and processes for creation of special account/donation to listed entities for unspent amount, as per law; and
- Keeping track of changes in relevant sections of the law and rules, and ensuring compliance.

The CSR leaders, on their part, need to deliver on commitments to the community, to work in close coordination with many internal departments to ensure that all compliances are met, and to push the spirit of the social responsibility agenda. They must be the evangelists for integrating social and environmental concerns in making business decisions. They must also be the bridge between those within the company and the non-profit partners, as hopefully they are familiar with both worlds.

One of the critical factors that CSR leaders need to ensure with the support of the senior management is that the they get clarity on the spend for any given financial year early on, so that plans may be prepared and approved at the earliest, giving enough time for proper implementation. The ideal time for planning for the next financial year is the last quarter of the current financial year. If plans and budgets are made and have internal approval by the end of March, the Board approvals for CSR activities can come through early in the financial year, and activities can proceed smoothly. However, this is a bit more complex than it sounds. While profits for two historical years are known, the profit for the current financial year is not available in March. This uncertainty sometimes delays the finalization of the CSR plan. Moreover, the approval of the plans depends on the scheduling of meetings of the CSR Committee and Board. If these get delayed, it has implications on the smooth progress of the CSR initiatives.

A useful mechanism in the context of proper internal coordination of CSR is the formation of a formal or informal committee involving the company secretary, finance department, the chartered accountant, and sometimes even the CEO's office. Such a forum is best steered by the CSR head and can help in shared understanding of the CSR priorities, commitments, deadlines, etc.

A CSR head must moreover make it a priority to:

- Keep on top of the law and rules, and every amendment,
- Set up internal coordination mechanisms,
- Maintain adequate communication with the CSR Committee,
- Get the CSR plan ready in time—well before 1 April (the possibility of designing initiatives as ongoing projects must be kept in mind in this process),
- Complete the selection of partner/s in time,
- Get approvals in time—preferably in April,
- Draw up proper MOUs with NGOs,
- Ensure that disbursements to implementing partners take place on time,
- Ensure proper orientation and building partner capacity,
- Monitor activities and budgets closely through the year and take timely action,
- Anticipate the need for an 'unspent amount' account, and open it in case needed,
- Ensure reporting in proper formats, and
- Draw up impact assessment TORs and identify good partners for this.

The biggest caution to the CSR manager is that this web of compliances, forms, formats, and reporting, should not lead to the organization losing the larger spirit of the activity, viz., making a difference to communities, and contributing to national development. Sometimes, the pressure towards compliance leads to a loss of focus on the initiatives and their impacts. Each team needs to have its own mechanism to be able to pull back from day-to-day activities and rededicate itself to the larger mission. And it should not lose the courage to experiment—CSR has been a space for innovation and experiments, and the stringent formats should not put paid to this.

Ironically, there is no explicit mention of the responsibilities of the CSR team in the law!

The Responsibilities of Auditors

While auditing of CSR activities has not been mandated, the various steps and processes do need monitoring to ensure that the letter and spirit of various provisions of the law are met. Proper disclosure of expenditures in the required formats has to be ensured. The accounting, recognition of expenditures and disclosures must be compliant with applicable accounting standards, and the transfers of unspent amounts must be done properly, etc. Moreover, when an outside implementing agency is carrying out CSR activities on behalf of a company, the expenses have to be certified by auditors, and independent practitioners have to give a report on utilization of CSR funds. Hence, auditors of both the company and the implementing agencies have a significant role in ensuring proper processes and compliances (for more on this see Institute of Chartered Accountants of India, 2020).

The Role of Employee Volunteering in CSR

Employee volunteering has been a pillar of CSR for decades now. Historically, volunteering has been seen as one of the benefits of an active CSR programme. It helps to boost employee morale—not only do employees feel good that their organization is concerned about the community, but it is also a source of satisfaction to get involved and put their skills and time into activities which make a difference in the lives of others. Volunteering helps corporate staff to understand societal realities and to develop empathy, as well as become aware of stakeholder concerns. It supports innovation, team building, leadership and organizational development. It reflects the organization's commitment towards socicty at large.

While employee volunteering is a critical part of CSR today, under the law it is not counted towards the mandated CSR spend. Nor can financial contributions by employees be counted as part of the spend. Nor does the law give any type of credit for employee contributions. It is not even a checkbox that a company has to tick in its list of CSR compliances. While urging corporates to encourage volunteering, the MCA has clarified that these cannot be monetized and shown as CSR contribution.

One would wish for a governmental stance that provided more of a nudge on this. However this lack of support should not, and fortunately has not, deterred companies from encouraging employee volunteering.

Such initiatives span a wide gamut. Sometimes the focus is on financial contributions. Payroll deduction is one method by which companies facilitate employees to donate money. Employees can opt to have a fixed amount deducted from their salaries every month and given to social causes. This may be to the company's own foundation, or it could be given to an external NGO that the company may have tied up with. This helps employees who have an urge to give but are hesitant because they are not aware of the credentials of various NGOs and whether their money will be used as they intended. By undertaking due diligence and monitoring, the company is able to certify the credibility of these organizations. In fact, payroll giving has evolved to an extent where there are specialized agencies which undertake the management of payroll deductions and donations.

Companies may also raise funds for specific causes or in response to specific events. For example, during disasters like Covid, floods, or earthquakes, companies have come up with diverse ways to help their employees to ensure that their donations reach the right hands. Sometimes, corporates match the donations of individual employees with their own contributions. In case of donations, employees typically look for income tax exemptions and hence, the company needs to facilitate mechanisms for providing the necessary receipts and certificates.

Some companies have tie-ups with NGOs to enable employees to go out into the community and engage in hands-on activities—teaching in a local school, counselling youth, helping organize a health camp, etc. Those with their own in-house foundations may create such opportunities within their own communities. Not just employees, many corporates encourage families of employees to get involved too. Several agencies are coming up to help volunteering at scale. Another venue for employee involvement is to work with government campaigns, e.g., encouraging staff to support the Pulse Polio endeavour, or Road Safety Week observances, etc.

Setting aside a day or days for community service is another popular method to encourage volunteering. Some multinationals have put into place a mechanism whereby their staff across countries and continents work towards this purpose on a designated day. The day may or may not be a working day. The cause may be the same across geographies—e.g., improving infrastructure of local schools, spending time with children in orphanages, or with senior citizens in assisted homes. Or the initiatives maybe locale-specific—e.g., in some countries it could be beach clean-up campaigns, in others it may be about painting and taking up repairs in government schools, and in yet others about creating awareness on endangered species.

A very meaningful way of volunteering is to enable employees to use their core skills to contribute to community development. For instance, the IT team can help develop apps for the needs of an associated foundation and NGOs; it can maintain computers in neighbouring government schools, and provide IT training for the teachers of these schools. Accounts departments can help NGOs improve their accounting systems. Finance teams can help in capacity building for communities on financial literacy, while HR teams can help through career counselling and career preparation inputs for local youth.

A few companies make community involvement and volunteering a part of the performance management system of their staff, even going to the extent of making it a criterion for promotions to senior management. Others have rewards and recognition systems. Volunteering gets a fillip when a company has a clear policy for this and the top management is seen to support this spirit. The arguments for companies to support, encourage, and facilitate voluntary involvement of staff are very strong, and hopefully Indian companies will continue to do this.

Box 7.2: Supporting the Spirit of Caring and Sharing

'Leader in Employee Volunteering' 2020

Tata Power has been recognized as a leader in facilitating employee volunteering. In 2020, over 2,500 employee volunteers contributed more than 28,000 volunteer hours. This was made possible by the structured approach the company takes towards employee volunteering. It has set up 'Arpan', an in-house portal for online volunteering, through which employees can find out about upcoming programmes and register themselves if they want to participate. The programmes focus on education, promotion of environmentally friendly practices, greening, and health, sanitation, and financial inclusion. Tata Power also has a robust rewards and recognition system to motivate their employee-volunteers.

Award by iVolunteer: https://ivolunteerawards.com/winners-2020/

8

Doing it Well

A strong implementation plan is at the core of effective and impactful CSR. In this context, it would be useful to review some tools and techniques that can help in various stages of planning and implementing CSR projects. Over the decades, the development sector has honed several processes for use at various stages of the project cycle, which would be useful in CSR contexts as well. Some of the tools developed in risk management and the ESG sector are useful for CSR operations too. A few commonly used tools are introduced below, with the proviso that each requires some amount of training and learning in order to be effectively used.

Some Tools and Techniques to Help Operationalize CSR

Preparatory Stage

Needs assessment

Before embarking on any CSR initiative, it is important to understand the needs of the community, and assess the assets therein. It is difficult to plan any activity without a strong understanding of ground realities and situations, and a needs assessment—a systematic process to find out the needs of a community, or to put it differently, the 'gaps' between the present situation and the desired situation—helps in this.

Needs assessment can help with the following:

- To determine the most important needs of the community, i.e., the critical development gaps,
- To prioritize these,
- To identify the goal of the proposed intervention, i.e., what 'closing the gap' would look like, and
- To identify and weigh alternative approaches or solutions.

The scope of a needs assessment must first be defined and the defined scope usually emerges from the corporate's policy as well as secondary data, informal feedback from the field, a rapid field assessment, expert opinion, etc. Nevertheless, how wide or narrow the scope is depends on the commissioning party. For instance, a corporate's CSR policy might simply be to 'work in the area of health'—a very large area for any needs assessment to cover. The community's key health issues, thrown up by this needs asessment, would then help the corporate to narrow down the areas in which it wants to work.

On the other hand, if the corporate's policy to 'work in the area of health' already includes specific target groups or thrust areas—such as maternal and child health, or the health of senior citizens, or mental health—the needs assessment would cover a smaller, clear-cut area. So knowing where one wants to go is important in deciding the scope of the needs assessment. Detailed assessment protocols are designed to get the information within the final framework of the scope. A needs assessment should use both secondary data from government and other sources, as well as primary data gathered through interviews, focus group discussions, surveys, observations, and group meetings. An external agency is usually hired to carry out the needs assessment, because an external perspective enhances objectivity and increases credibility of decisions that follow. A sample of a Preliminary Needs Assessment is given in Annexure 2.

Stakeholder analysis

Stakeholders are usually defined as 'people, groups, or institutions, which are likely to be affected by a proposed project (either negatively or positively), or those which can affect the outcome of the project' (Rietbergen-McCracken and Narayan. 1998). Stakeholders may be principally categorized into: (a) primary stakeholders, who are directly affected by or affect the initiative, e.g., investors, employees, customers, vendors, local communities ; and, (b) secondary stakeholders, who play indirect or intermediary roles which could have significant effects on the outcomes of the project. Secondary stakeholders may include local government, NGOs, media, etc. Both types of stakeholders can affect initiatives positively or negatively.

Stakeholder analysis is important for any development project, but is especially critical for CSR initiatives, and needs to take into account the stakeholders of the specific CSR intervention, and of the business operation. A key factor in the context of a CSR project is that stakeholder dynamics are more complicated than if an NGO were independently taking up the same activity in the community. The stakeholder analysis must also keep in mind that stakeholder expectations from the business are usually high and are often projected on to CSR activities. For instance, a faction within a village may have certain expectations from the business or may be opposed to it for some reason. Since members of the faction may not be able to make their voices heard in other fora, they may oppose CSR activities as a way of signalling their point of view. Hence, a wide view has to be taken of stakeholders.

The key steps in stakeholder analysis are:

- Identification of key stakeholders, and their grouping;
- Assessing interests and the potential impact of each group of stakeholders on the proposed project; and
- Prioritizing stakeholders in terms of their power and impact on the CSR initiative.

Based on the analysis, a Stakeholder Management Plan should be developed which clarifies how to overcome any challenges that may crop up; how to mitigate opposition and increase support for the initiative. As interests of stakeholders may change over time, adjustments to the plan will be needed from time to time, and this flexibility should be articulated in the plan.

A sample stakeholder analysis is given in Annexure 3. The highlighted portions in the sample stem from the corporate connection of the development intervention. In other words, if a neutral NGO were to undertake the same activity, it may not encounter these factors.

Materiality mapping

In the context of sustainability strategy, reporting and risk management, 'materiality' may be understood as 'relevance'. A material issue is one, as per the Global Reporting Initiative, which has the 'potential to significantly affect sustainability performance' (www.globalreporting.org). It may be an economic, environmental, or social issue on which a company has an impact, or by which it may be impacted. It is an issue which is not only important to a company, but can also significantly influence the assessments and decisions of stakeholders. Taking into account materiality as part of the planning exercise ensures that issues critical for sustainability are addressed.

An accepted best practice in sustainability reporting is that a company should report on the relevant or 'material' issues that have a direct or indirect impact on its being able to create, maintain, or reduce value for its stakeholders, the environment, and society at large. Hence, as part of the CSR/sustainability planning exercise, it is important to gain an understanding of materiality, and plan the CSR initiatives to respond to these. This will help to make the interventions more meaningful and strategic.

Let us consider an example. The issue of air pollution may be considered material for thermal power plants. Such air pollution may affect the health of workers at the plant and local communities around the plant. If a power plant is perceived to be polluting by the local community, it may face opposition from stakeholder groups. Thus air pollution is material to such a company's corporate and sustainability efforts. Or to take another example, if a manufacturing facility is heavily dependent on groundwater resources, there is a possibility that availability of water for the local community will reduce through its operations. This is a material issue and the response may be to work towards groundwater recharge.

Generally, the process for conducting a materiality assessment includes the following steps:

- Identifying key issues related to sustainability, and categorizing those relevant;
- Collecting data from internal and external stakeholders about their priorities with regard to these issues;

- Mapping and prioritizing issues;
- Aligning issues with management, business, and CSR vision; and
- Developing strategy.

CSR Project Planning Tools and Techniques

The international development system including UN agencies, World Bank, Dept. for International Development, Govt. of UK (DFID), etc., have evolved several project-planning tools, and these are increasingly being deployed in CSR too. Some frequently used techniques are briefly described below.

Baseline data collection

This is a critical step to start the planning process. It is collection of the data relevant to the intervention at the present point in time, before the intervention. For instance, if the plan is to improve employability of youth, the agency needs to know for sure what the situation is now. In this case, it would start with: How many youth are there in the target age group? How many boys, how many girls? What are their education and skill levels? How many of them are working? What type of work? How much are they earning? What is the nature of work—permanent, contractual, casual, with benefits, without benefits? Without a good handle on such data, it is difficult to plan any intervention, and almost impossible to evaluate it.

Theory of Change (TOC) and Log Frame (LF)

TOC and LF are both planning tools which help visualize how to get from the current situation to the desired situation, with a focus on:

- Understanding and analysing the assumptions being made,
- Setting down a systematic process to achieve goals, and
- Laying down parameters to tell us how we know whether we are getting there.

Theory of Change

Usually, the TOC is formulated first and then the LF. TheTOC tries to capture the complex processes involved in social change in any given context. It tries to describe how and why a desired change is likely to take place. It specifically pays attention to mapping out or 'filling in' what has been described as the 'missing middle'—the gap between what a programme or change initiative does (its activities or interventions), and how these lead to the desired goals being achieved.

The TOC process starts by identifying long-term goals and works back from these to identify all the conditions (outcomes) that must be in place for the goals to be achieved; and also how these conditions relate to one another in terms of cause and effect. All these are plotted on an 'outcomes framework', which results in a better understanding of the link between activities and the achievement of the long-term goals.

As per UK Aid Connect (n.d.), TOC:

- Maps out multiple causal pathways,
- Explores what is implicit—spelling out assumptions,
- Cites the evidence (or lack of it) relating to each causal link,
- Prompts critical reflection and rethinking of approach, and
- Is of particular value for evaluation.

Figure 8.1: Simplified TOC for Sustainable Livelihoods Enhancement Project

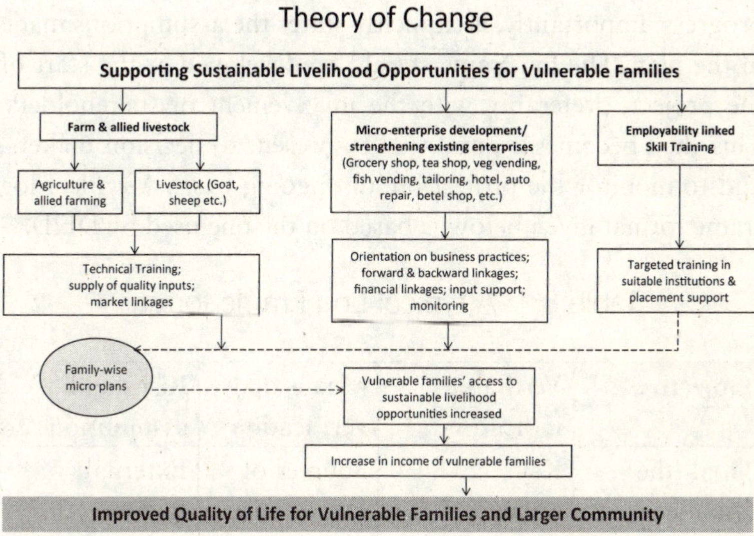

Log Frame Analysis

Also called the 'logical framework analysis' (shortened to log frame or LFA), it is used for planning and managing development projects. It is drawn up like a table (or framework) and presents information about the critical components of the initiative in a logical and systematic way.

The DFID, one of the pioneers of this technique says that 'Logframes have great value in clarifying thinking about the task to be achieved and how to evaluate change. They also have value as a means of improving communication between participants in any given activity' (DFID 2003).

LFA is a logical way of putting down the plan in a format which forces the project team to think through the assumptions, causalities, and steps in the project process. It helps monitor progress against plans, and incorporates baseline data as well as indicators, targets, and sources of information to gauge progress. Importantly, it explicitly states the assumptions made in the plan. The log frame should be developed at the start of the project, preferably with the involvement of stakeholders. This then becomes a good tool to present to decision makers, and to monitor the project on an ongoing basis. A typical log frame format given below is based on the one used by DFID.

Table 8.1: A typical Log Frame format

Objectives	Verifiable indicators	Means of verification	Risks and assumptions
Goal (the broader impact to which the project will contribute)	Key indicators related to overall goals	Sources of information of these indicators	External factors necessary to sustain objectives in the long term
Purpose/s (the immediate development outcome at the end of the project)	Indicators which clearly show that the objectives of the actions have been achieved	Sources of information that exist or can be collected Methods required to collect this information	Factors and external conditions to achieve the objective

Objectives	Verifiable indicators	Means of verification	Risks and assumptions
Output/s (specifically deliverable results envisaged to achieve the specific objectives)	Indicators to show whether and to what extent the action achieves the expected results	Sources of information for these indicators	External conditions needed to deliver the results in the required time frame
Activities (key activities to be carried out and their sequences, in order to achieve the expected results)	Means required to perform these activities, e.g., HR, finances, infra etc.	Sources of information about the progress of activities What are the action costs?	Preconditions required before action starts

Source: Based on log frame by DFID, as seen at https://www.gdrc.org/ngo/logical-fa.pdf

Results Based Management

The UN system uses result-based management (RBM) for most of its development projects at the country level. The UN defines RBM as

> A management strategy by which all actors, contributing directly or indirectly to achieving a set of results, ensure that their processes, products and services contribute to the desired results (outputs, outcomes and higher level

> goals or impact) and use information and evidence on actual results to inform decision making on the design, resourcing and delivery of programmes and activities as well as for accountability and reporting (UNDG, 2011).

Like TOC and LFA, RBM also focuses on taking a systematic approach to the chain of events leading to a change, and maps out the following at the start of the project, and then monitors them through the project cycle. RBM looks at

- Outcomes and outputs;
- Indicators, baselines, and targets;
- Means of verification;
- Risks and assumptions;
- Role of partners, and
- Indicative resources needed (e.g., finances, HR resources, etc.). (ibid.).

The Ultimate Test: Measuring Impact

Recent amendments to the CSR Rules in India mandate that certain size of projects be formally evaluated through an external agency. Even apart from this, as per the 2013 Act, the CSR policy itself is required to ensure that there be 'monitoring process of such projects or programs'. With more resources being spent on CSR and more being demanded from it, rigorous monitoring and evaluation are taking on greater significance. Any corporate would like to know whether the money and effort it is putting into CSR is having the desired impacts or not.

Monitoring and evaluation are well-developed fields within the development sector and are integral parts of any well-designed projects. To quickly understand the difference between the two, monitoring is an ongoing process during project implementation. Evaluation on the other hand, is taken up periodically, usually at some important milestone or once a project has been completed.

Fundamental to any monitoring and evaluation are proper baseline data, management information systems (MIS), and documentation (see Annexure 4). As a part of the project design it is important to decide what data is important, and create the design for capturing it in the granularity and frequency required. These will emerge from TOC or LFA processes, and CSR project managers need to ensure that they give proper structure to the capturing of the necessary data.

Monitoring: 'Are we doing the project correctly?'

Through monitoring, management can be alerted to any challenges in the process of implementation. Monitoring looks at the process through which inputs and activities result in outputs. It helps to track whether inputs are available when they are needed, and whether they are being properly used. Monitoring is a way of becoming aware of any deviations from expected results, so that the team can introspect on causes of error and identify corrective actions needed to once again align a project's path to its target. Monitoring is an integral part of the project design, and is usually done by the team itself, with reviews by the management. Feedback from beneficiaries may be a part of the monitoring.

Some initiatives look at two levels of monitoring, viz., 'results monitoring', which looks at how well the project is contributing to its objectives; and 'implementation monitoring', viz., how effectively and efficiently the project is delivering the results. For instance, implementation monitoring may look at

- Physical delivery of goods and services;
- The use of goods and services by the target population (outputs), and
- The management of financial resources.

While results monitoring may focus on

- The progress of the project towards achieving the project purpose, and
- The impact of the project on different groups of people

Evaluation

Evaluation adopts a broader perspective than monitoring—its aim is to understand progress towards achieving a project's larger purpose and end goal. It looks at issues of the impact and relevance of an initiative, the design of a project, and how efficiently it is carried out. A holistic evaluation thus looks at the following five criteria: impact, relevance, effectiveness, efficiency, and sustainability.

While there is no laid-down timetable, mid-term and end-of-project evaluations may be conducted for large projects, and only at end-of-project for others. Some evaluations may be done long after the end-of-project—for instance, when measuring long-term impacts of providing scholarships at high-school level, an evaluation could be conducted five years after the scholarships were given.

Evaluations are usually anchored by people who have not been involved in the initiative. Sometimes, members of the internal/ implementing group may be part of the evaluation team. Evaluations are generally done by interdisciplinary teams, to get a holistic, comprehensive, and balanced picture of the impacts of the initiatives. For instance, if it is a sanitation project, the team may include civil or sanitation engineers, gender specialists, communications persons, social change experts, etc.

Even when external evaluations are not being carried out, it is still important that at least an internal team does a formal evaluation of significant CSR initiatives at set intervals. There could be an internal policy regarding this, e.g., all programmes will be evaluated once in five years.

A useful practice adopted by some companies is to create an internal interdisciplinary team for this, with people from various departments (from strategy to marketing to CSR) of the company. This can help to bring new perspectives into the social development processes.

Impact assessment: Only for projects of a certain size and above

The law in India specifies that impact assessment needs to be undertaken for specified size of CSR spends and projects. The purpose of doing this, as per the Ministry of Corporate Affairs is to

> [...] assess the social impact of a particular CSR project. The intent is to encourage companies to take considered decisions before deploying CSR amounts and assess the impact of their CSR spending. This not only serves as feedback for companies to plan and allocate resources better but shall also deepen the impact of CSR.
>
> (See '19.0 Impact Assessment' in FAQ table; Ministry of Corporate Affairs, 2021)

The World Health Organization (WHO) defines impact assessment as being, 'the process link in the chain between evidence and decision-making'. (https://www.who.int/heli/impacts/en/)

As per the Organization for Economic Co-operation and Development (OECD), 'the essence of impact analysis is to establish such a supposed chain of causation ("theory") from intervention to impact and to measure or describe the changes induced along that chain' (OECD, n.d.).

Impact assessment is an integral part of such frameworks as LFA, and follows from them. It is however very large in its scope. In practical terms, there is an apprehension in the CSR community whether it will really be possible to carry out 'impact assessments' as mandated, or whether it will basically just be evaluations that are done to fulfil this requirement.

Social Return on Investment (SROI)

A powerful tool to understand the value created by an initiative, SROI recognizes that all actions create or destroy value beyond what can be stated in financial terms, and hence the approach is designed to go beyond looking at just financial value creation, towards including social and environmental value in the calculation. It is '… an evaluation methodology that uses the outcomes of a given activity to understand and quantify the "value" that it creates – or destroys – in economic, social and environmental terms' (Social Change UK).' SROI '…measures changes in ways that are relevant to people and/or organizations that experience or contribute to it. It tells the story of how change is being created by measuring the social, environmental and economic outcomes, using monetary values to represent them' (SROI Network, 2012). It has the advantage that it talks in terms of return on investment (ROI), a term which businesses are familiar and comfortable with.

Take the example of giving scholarships to poor and meritorious girls to undertake professional studies. One benefit is obvious and easily quantifiable—the increase in economic earning power. But there are many other benefits which one has to consider in order to arrive at the final total benefit. For instance, the girl may support her younger siblings to get a better education, and that has its own benefit streams. The girl may become a role model and inspire other girls in her community to aspire for professional jobs. She may defer an early marriage. Thus SROI facilitates the effort to think through all such benefits and to express them all in monetary terms (as far as possible), and thus arrive at a conclusion about the value addition. Based on social accounting and cost–benefit analysis, SROI is stated in ratio terms, i.e., what was the cost vs the total social value of an investment. For instance, a ratio of 3:1 means that an input of Re 1 achieved a social value of Rs 3.

Lawlor et al. (2009) define the principles underpinning SROI as

- Involve stakeholders,
- Understand what changes,
- Value the things that matter,
- Only include what is material,
- Do not over-claim,
- Be transparent, and
- Verify the result.

Thus SROI is a powerful tool, and it is worthwhile for any CSR team to spend time on understanding it and applying it to their initiatives. However, while an internal exercise is useful, SROI can be confusing for beginners. Many assumptions have to be made, which need to be discussed and understood. Hence, it is recommended that the process of developing this should be facilitated by experts, at least initially. Since it is a tool gaining increasing importance, a simple internal SROI exercise is given as a sample in Annexure 4.

As in SROI, so too with the other tools and techniques outlined in this chapter—they all require specialized knowledge and expertise. While it is useful to develop these in-house, it may be a good idea to have some of these processes facilitated by external experts.

9
Of Proposals and Partners

A lot of time is spent on discussing two components of CSR implementation within any company, namely, CSR proposals, and CSR partners.

Even more is spent in NGOs on these topics! This chapter tries to outline the processes in a way that hopes to be helpful to both parties.

Proposals for CSR activities may be drawn up in different contexts. For instance, an NGO may put an unsolicited proposal before a company; a company may request an NGO for a proposal; the CSR department of the company or its foundation may have to prepare a proposal for the senior management or the CSR Committee and the Board. The approaches have to be somewhat different for each of these situations.

Implementing partners are parts of the project cycle in different ways. Some may come in to implement entire projects, some to carry out specified activities within an overall programme, some to do a needs assessment or an evaluation.

But a company needs to give serious thought to its partnerships, just as much as an outside agency desiring to become a partner in a company's CSR journey has to.

Both NGOs and corporates have to study and be fully aware of every nuance of the legal requirements. For instance, an NGO needs to be aware of the basis of CSR spend calculations, the CSR policy of the company they are approaching, etc. A corporate has to be aware of whom they can take on board as implementation partner/s.

It is important both for the corporate and the implementing partner to be comfortable on the fundamentals. Does each respect and trust the other? Are the value systems compatible? Is there a match in the broad vision of social development in general and CSR in particular? Are both sides comfortable with the contours of the partnership? It would be very difficult to go ahead without this compatibility. During the process of initial meetings, it is important for both sides to ascertain this and go ahead only if this meeting of minds seems to exist. It is easy to get into a partnership but often difficult to sustain and live it.

This chapter looks at some aspects of these discussions.

Key Elements of a CSR Proposal

Proactive Proposals from Implementing Agencies

Often an NGO puts in a proposal to a company seeking to partner it. Such a proposal by the NGO may seek support for its own ongoing activities, in the geographies where it already is working. Such proposals may meet with success if the NGO is working on one of the company's selected thrust areas, in the company's geographic priority area. They may also be viewed positively by corporates who are geography-agnostic, i.e., an IT company which considers the whole country its operational area and is thus open to working anywhere. If the NGO is working on a cause which is a national mission at that moment, or the NGO is a very large one, or whose credibility is known personally to top decision makers—in such cases also, the proposals may be considered seriously. However, it seems that as times go by, such proposals may find it increasingly difficult to find support.

Another scenario may be that an NGO is doing excellent work in one state. It may propose extension of its activities into the company's desired geographies. This may meet with success when the NGO is well known and has a proven track record of expertise in a thematic area of interest to the company and falling within its CSR policy. Also, this is likely to succeed when the work involves some specialized expertise which the corporate/foundation does not have, and is difficult or expensive to build—for instance, provision of specialized medical services.

Yet another possibility is that an NGO may be suggesting that it can help the company implement whole or part of its ongoing CSR programmes. Such proposals may be considered if the NGO has a strong grass-roots presence in the geography of the company's interest as well as a holistic approach and capacity. Usually a company would like to take up CSR across more than one thematic area, e.g., education, health, and poverty alleviation. If the NGO has a track record of community connect, and the ability to carry out the programmes in all these thematic work areas, the proposal may be considered favourably.

Any such proposal will have a better chance if the NGO understands the needs of the corporate and clearly articulates how it can offer value to the corporate which will be synergistic, and accordingly designs and develops its proposals. A company has its own priorities, challenges and interest areas—proposals which factor these in are likely to be taken up positively. So any proposal has to start with a deep study of the company's CSR policy, processes, philosophy, etc. Apart from the information that can be gleaned from the company website, it would be useful for an NGO to reach out to the corporate before it starts preparing the proposal, and have an in-depth discussion.

The NGO also needs to be aware of the CSR cycle of the company. Usually, the CSR proposals are approved in the first quarter of the year. Hence, the timing of putting in proposals is also important.

It must be borne in mind that while there is provision for multi-year projects (one plus three years long, i.e., the year of the proposal and three years following), CSR approvals are usually on an annual cycle and they need to be monitored on an annual cycle. Hence even though the programme may be long-term in nature, any proposal should clearly indicate the outcomes, outputs, and budgets on an annual basis.

In the case of an NGO or external agency applying to a corporate without a prior relationship, the proposal needs to be quite detailed in all aspects. It is important for the NGOs to demonstrate their organizational credibility and governance systems, their understanding of CSR and the corporate, the quality of their staff, their commitment level, their programme management skills including monitoring, evaluation, and reporting, and of course their ability to deliver the desired impacts.

Proposals Solicited by a Company

Sometimes, a company may reach out to an NGO for help in its CSR mission. There are two scenarios even within this. The first situation is when there is a general call for proposals. Qualifying NGOs can apply and then go through a competitive selection process. In such cases, the frameworks and formats are clearly given, and the NGO has to ensure to fill these with care.

In the second situation, a company may approach a local or well-known NGO to take up specific tasks or help it implement its overall programme. In such cases, there will be opportunity for detailed discussion between the corporate and the NGO, and a mutually comfortable proposal can be worked out.

Box 9.1: Delivering Impact through NGO Partners

HCL Foundation, HCL's CSR arm, has a unique angle to its CSR programmes, whereby it strengthens and empowers NGOs through one of the biggest institutionalized CSR grants in India. It supports breakthrough and highly impactful projects undertaken by NGOs working in environment, health, and education, which address the needs of marginalized, isolated, underserved and underdeveloped rural communities in India

Based on a rigorous seven-step selection process, one NGO in each category—environment, health, and education—receives a grant of Rs 5 crore for a three-to-five year project. Two finalists in each category receive a grant of Rs 25 lakh for year-long projects.

Started in 2015, the HCL Grant has already committed Rs 78.67 crore towards high-impact projects by NGOs that have a proven track record of impact, credibility, and ability to deliver.

Based on www.hclfoundation.org

Critical Elements in a CSR Proposal

The following are some points that would be important for an NGO to cover in its proposal.

Organizational credibility

There are several aspects of credibility including expertise, experience, and track record to deliver the committed project objectives and make an impact; governance and management; robustness of systems and processes; and the people associated with it and its existing partners. Finances, sources of funds, and accounts are also key elements that companies look into.

Some of the key documents which help to establish these and therefore need to be attached to a proposal include: audited financial reports, annual activity reports, details of significant projects completed, the details of Board members, any significant awards or recognitions, etc. Form CSR 1 is now essential for any CSR implementing agency, and it would be important to attach this permission, apart from the registration certificate, PAN, 80G and 12A. If the entity has 35 AC and FCRA (Foreign Contribution Regulation Act, 1976) certificates, these too maybe attached.

Understanding CSR requirements and the company

It is important to understand the legal requirements of acting as a CSR implementing agency and it must be demonstrated in the proposal that the organization fits the criteria.

It would be necessary for the NGO to thoroughly understand the company's CSR policy and way of working, and identify possible synergies, before setting to work on the proposal. For instance, what are the company's selected thrust areas from among the permissible activities in Schedule VII? In which geographies does it prefer to take up CSR? Who are its existing partners? Companies are also increasingly wanting to ensure volunteering opportunities for staff, and a proposal needs to take these into consideration. Without being well aware of such background information, the chances of success for the external agency may be slim.

Showcasing capabilities

A corporate seeks NGO partners because it believes that they will be able to bring about the socio-economic development it wants to see. Therefore a project proponent must demonstrate its ability to successfully carry out and deliver the promised impacts and outcomes. For this, it needs to talk about its track record; the partners it has worked with; the depth, width, strength, and qualifications of its staff; the systems and processes it has in place; how it undertakes monitoring and evaluation of its projects; and any impact evaluation reports of its initiatives. Since reporting and financial management are key, it must also showcase these capabilities. A mention of the awards and recognitions it has won is also appropriate.

Delivery of results

In terms of the proposed programme, the partner's capabilities in the corporate's areas of interest—both thematic and geographical—must be demonstrated. Since CSR underspending is a serious issue, the proposal must clearly demonstrate that the agency has the bandwidth and will deploy the resources necessary to carry out the activities and spends as proposed. The proposal must also lay down outcomes, milestones, and results clearly. The budget heads must be transparent. Reporting requirements expected from a corporate with regard to CSR are stringent, and hence the implementing agency must make clear commitments on these. The SROI or cost–benefit analysis of the proposed activities may be included.

Governance

This is the aspect that many corporates are deeply concerned with. The implementing agency must highlight the people associated with it at Board and senior management levels, the systems and processes it has in place for financial and programme management, its HR practices, etc.

It gives credibility if its partnerships with any other corporates or reputed bodies are mentioned. Hence it should also highlight its accreditations or affiliations which demonstrate its credentials (see subsection 'Credibility Checks').

Proposals from Internal Foundation or CSR Department

A core function of the CSR Committee and the Board is to go into the details of the CSR proposal for the year, approve it and monitor its implementation. Hence even if the implementation is done in-house, it is necessary to have a proposal with all implementation details. While an internal proponent may not need to go into too much detail regarding organizational credibility, track record of performance, etc., it is a good practice to make every document complete in itself. To this end—and keeping in view that the CSR Committee and the Board do have independent members and that members may change—providing basic information and background does help better reception of the proposal.

An internal proponent has the advantage of knowing the priorities for the upcoming year, as well as the exact CSR budget mandated for that year. Hence, it can tailor the proposal accordingly. Depending on the corporate's resources, if needed, more than the mandatory budget may also be allocated. It would be a good idea for the internal CSR unit to discuss the budget with the senior management beforehand and make plans based on this. Internal proposals also need to take into account any underspending in the previous year and specifically discuss the treatment of the leftover funds. Similar is the case of multi-year projects.

If the internal department or the foundation is working with NGOs to implement some or all of the CSR activities, these proposals must be incorporated into the proposal being put up.

Elements of a Good Proposal and its Evaluation

Whether it is a proposal from an NGO or the company's own department or in-house foundation, the senior management, CSR Committee, and the Board need to ensure that the proposal falls within the legislation, fits the company's policy, vision, and priorities, matches the resource availability, addresses important and current community needs, and that it will deliver the promised results effectively and efficiently.

A CSR proposal should therefore include the following details:

- Needs analysis,
- Rationale of the proposal and how it fits the CSR vision,
- Geographic area of implementation (including state and districts),
- Objectives,
- Activities and their fit to Schedule VII,
- Implementation details,
- Relevant baseline data,
- Theory of change/log frame,

- Outputs and outcomes,
- Timelines and milestones,
- Monitoring mechanisms, and how the impacts will be measured,
- Budgets and spending plans, and
- Reporting protocols.

If the company is itself implementing CSR, it needs to ensure that not more than 5 per cent of the budget will be spent on administration (as defined before). It would be a good idea to refer to the reporting format in the MCA notification of 22 January 2021, and to ensure that the proposal has all the required information to be able to fill this at the end of the year. Through the year, it is important to keep the CSR Committee and the Board apprised of the progress of the project, and to seek approval for changes to the proposal if needed.

Processes to evaluate CSR proposals

In-house and external proposals are of course likely to be processed differently. However, all project proponents need to provide the CSR Committee and the Board with all the information required to help them make decisions. Proposal evaluation usually takes place in several stages.

Below is an overview of typical processes under different scenarios.

Applications against call for proposals

As mentioned earlier, in some cases corporates have large grants for which they call for proposals, maybe in a thematic area or geography. There is a set format for these proposals and a timeline. There is usually a multistage process and evaluation committees at various stages. Putting one's proposal through such a rigorous process is very helpful even if one fails to get the grant, as it helps to identify weak areas—whether in governance, systems, processes, or planning. Equally, it helps to understand one's strengths. It helps an NGO become aware of what others are doing and how. These ultimately prove as forums for learning and sharing, which help in the long run.

Standard Process for Other NGO Proposals

The following is likely to be the process for most NGO proposals, though in situations where the company has asked a particular NGO to put in a proposal and there have been detailed discussions, many of the requirements are likely to have been met. However, the broad process may be as below.

Scrutiny by CSR team and management

In case the CSR team itself has called on a specific NGO for a proposal, it may be assumed that they have ascertained the details about the organization and its programme capabilities. Otherwise, there would be a deep dive into these aspects. Whichever route the proposal comes through, the company's CSR team will do the preliminary work of due diligence—checking the proposal against the requirements of the legislation, the company CSR policy, and current priorities. The following may be looked into.

Compliance with the law

The implementing partner should be registered as a trust, society, or Section 8 company, and should have a three-year track record of activities of the same nature as proposed. It should have 80G and 12A certificates. The registration of any CSR implementing agency with the Ministry of Corporate Affairs, using Form CSR 1 is essential.

Credibility checks

The scrutinizing team may go through the background of the CSR implementing agency, its experience, governance record, etc. They may look into audited annual reports of the last few years. Going beyond the papers, they may want to understand its systems, processes, and governance practices. If the CSR implementing agency is an NGO, the CSR team may check the accreditation of the NGO on various platforms like GiveIndia, GuideStar, etc. The CSR team would be networked within the development community and may also check with peers and networks about the NGO as part of the reference check. The risk to reputation via association with an agency is fairly high on the mind of a corporate, and they would try to ensure that the association is risk-free.

Companies may also scrutinize blacklists, such as those of the Council for Action and Rural Technology (CAPART) and other government ministries and departments, as part of their due diligence.

Strength of proposal

The CSR team may have a preliminary discussion with the NGO on the project. Since they are the ones working on the subject of social development, they will examine the objectives, processes, and proposed outcomes, maybe through a log frame. They may give inputs to the NGO for strengthening the proposal. They will probably check the budget as to whether it is reasonable. They may pay special attention to administrative costs, as this is a major area of attention of committees. (Once again it must be stressed that the 5 per cent cap on administrative expenses does not apply to implementing partners, but funders are always sensitive to this cost head!) In case the NGO has worked with the corporate before, obviously the previous performance would be taken into consideration.

The proposal may be rejected at this stage if it does not meet the criteria or is not aligned with the company's objectives. Or the company may ask for a rework. Or they may ask for the proposal to be put into a particular format for placing before the CSR Committee.

Credits

The credit for CSR activities is obviously shared between the company and the implementing agency. However, it would be useful during the preliminary discussions itself for the corporate and the NGO to clarify and document this. This is not just about publicity. For instance, a company would like the goodwill of the community. This must be the collateral benefit of its taking up development activities in its (the corporate's) neighbourhood. So if only the name of an NGO comes to the fore in all the community activities, it will not be appreciated by the company. If great work is happening in a district with regard to drinking water or schools under its CSR, the corporate needs the district authorities to be aware of this.

This is often a reason why corporates prefer their own in-house foundations, as the link of the good work to the parent company is obvious for all stakeholders. So all aspects of the credit—from banners to hoardings to branding to communication in the community—need to be discussed and agreed. While these may not be put down in the proposal, there should be a broad agreement.

Review by senior management

Sometimes, after discussion within the CSR team, if it is a large proposal, it may be put up to the CEO or the senior management who may have to defend it in front of the Board.

Recommendation by CSR Committee

The next step is that the CSR Committee looks into the proposal of the NGO. Usually it gives significant weight to the recommendations of the CSR team. The CSR Committee naturally wants to assure itself that the proposal fits into the larger mission/vision; that the NGO will deliver on its promises; that the costs justify the outcomes; and that in no case will there be a risk to reputation. Based on these considerations, the CSR Committee makes a recommendation to the Board. (In case the company is not required to have a CSR Committee, the proposal is put up directly to the Board for approval.)

Approval by Board

The CSR Committee places the proposal before the Board with its recommendations. The Board usually has more or less the same considerations as the CSR Committee, and may ask the CSR Committee whether due diligence has been carried out with regard to these considerations. Based on the CSR Committee's assurances, the Board gives its approval. In case the company does not have a CSR Committee because it is not required to, the Board will spend more time discussing and approving the proposal.

Standard Process for Proposals of Internal CSR Department or Foundation

The scrutiny for an internal proposal may be different but no less intense. The expectations from an internal unit may be even higher!

Usually, the CSR team would develop its proposals based on its understanding of the community needs and the available funds. That said, it is not entirely unknown for a programme idea to trickle down from top, say the CEO or an independent member of the Board. Even so, the CSR team needs to go through somewhat similar processes if only to ensure that the programme fits into the overall framework of their CSR activities.

Once the proposal is ready, the process may typically proceed as follows:

Internal review

The CEO or senior team will review the previous year's performance and the current year's proposal, and give inputs based on changed priorities, budgets, etc. The team would rework accordingly.

Review by CSR Committee

The first year when a policy is made, discussions may be detailed in order to develop a shared understanding of priorities, operationalization, team capabilities, effectiveness and efficiency, process, etc. In subsequent years, the CSR Committee may spend more time on discussing the changing business environment and its impacts on the proposal. It will want to discuss past performance and may go into whether the initiative is delivering the promised impacts, and suggest project evaluations. Following that, unlcss there are major changes, the CSR Committee would ascertain that the proposal is on the right lines and meets current priorities. Based on this, it would make a recommendation to the Board.

The CSR Committee may focus considerable attention on progress of multi-year proposals. It would be particularly concerned in case it spots any risks of not achieving the mandatory spend. In case the company is not required to have a CSR Committee, these responsibilities would be directly undertaken by the Board.

Approval by the Board

The CSR Committee presents the proposals to the Board with its recommendations. The Board, having ascertained that the CSR Committee has looked in detail into the broader perspective of the proposal, would give its approval.

Partnerships—Key to Impactful CSR

At various stages of the CSR cycle, corporates need to work with outside agencies—whether it is for conducting needs assessment or project implementation, or carrying out evaluations, etc. How can they go about selecting partners? The following discussions may help throw some light on this.

The governmental accreditation of NGOs and CSR implementation partners have both been frequently discussed, but there is no official system in place yet. NGO Darpan—a website maintained under the aegis of the Niti Aayog—lists over one lakh voluntary organizations, classified state-wise and with their thrust areas of activities. However, it comes with the caution that the listing is, 'based on self-declared information. This does not imply that organizations are endorsed or recommended by the NITI Aayog / MeitY-NIC or by the concerned Ministries/Departments/Government Bodies' (ngodarpan.gov.in).

Registration of implementing partners with the Ministry of Corporate Affairs through CSR Form 1 is now compulsory. However, this gives assurance only of some basic credentials—essentially the nature of the entity, that the entity is registered, has a Permanent Account number (PAN), and details about its directors. It gives no idea about its capabilities beyond the fact that it has carried out relevant programmes for the last three years. In this scenario, the selection of an NGO for implementing CSR projects poses some challenges.

Nothing can take the place of due diligence by the corporate. Everything, from closely studying the annual reports, visiting the organization and its field activities, and talking to stakeholders is important. Consultation with peer CSRs and other funders will also give some directions. Some corporates which work with a large number of partners have formalized frameworks for such due diligence. Fortunately, there are sources which can help the companies understand potential partners more deeply. Some major ones are mentioned below.

Credibility Alliance

This is an alliance of NGOs which came together over twenty years ago to draw up 'Minimum Norms for Good Governance, Accountability and Transparency of the Voluntary Sector' through wide-ranging consultations. Now NGOs can get themselves accredited through this, and it provides assurance of governance and process.

CRISIL's VO (Voluntary Organization) Grading

Another well-recognized process, it uses a '4P' framework, looking at 'profile, process, programme, and proficiency', and the process to arrive at the grading 'includes document verification, management discussion, field visits, in-depth analysis of financial and performance data' (www.crisil.com). It uses a matrix approach to slot VOs in terms of Financial Proficiency and Delivery Capability, and takes into account a comprehensive set of relevant factors, from governance and management to programme implementation and cost structure.

CSRBox

A platform for all matters CSR, it also has a section where it lists potential partners categorized into three sections—vetted partners, verified organizations, and those 'under verification'.

GiveIndia platform

This is another credible forum to check. It reviews and weighs hundreds of non-profit organizations from all over India against its list of well-developed assurance criteria, as part of the process of putting them on its platform as eligible recipients of donations through its site. This assurance is helpful for a corporate looking for an implementation partner. If an NGO is on the GiveIndia platform, it is definitely a level of assurance.

GuideStar India

This is an initiative of Civil Society Information Services India which is a trust. It is an aggregator of information about NGOs and has an online database of reliable and comparable information on over 10,000 NGOs, over 1,400 of which have undergone varying levels of due diligence. GuideStar India also has a much larger offline database.

GlobalGiving

An international platform, it undertakes rigorous duc diligence on every organization it lists. The database lists several hundred Indian NGOs.

Apart from these, there are also some helpful sectoral pointers available. For instance, if a company is looking for a skill-training partner, it would make sense to check if the organization is implementing programmes for National Skill Development Corporation (NSDC), or the Ministry of Rural Development, or State Skill Missions, etc., as all of these have their own due diligence processes in place.

Operationalizing the Partnership

Once the partners have agreed to work with each other, there is still the issue of how the partnership should be formalized. The easiest structure for a corporate and NGO to work together might be for the corporate to enter into a grant agreement with the NGO. Service contracts are more complicated, and involve payment of taxes. From the NGO perspective, there is also a cap on the percentage of its earnings that can come from providing services. Grant agreements obviate these problems.

A grant is like a donation, except that conditionalities can be included in the grant agreement (for example, specific deliverables, timelines, budget details, etc.). It would be useful for a corporate to draw up a model agreement, get it vetted not only by its legal and finance departments but also by a few of its partners with whom it has been working in a CSR relationship. Such partners would help ensure that the model agreement is more 'equal' and fair to both the corporate and the potential implementing partners. A critical element would also be to share and discuss draft agreements with partners who are coming on board, and take in their legitimate concerns and modify the agreements as needed.

Towards a Win-Win Corporate–NGO Relationship

Today, even as corporates are setting up their foundations to carry out CSR, the relationship between corporates and NGOs is deepening, and there is an effort from both sides to understand the other's point of view and to strive for win-win partnerships. There are several barriers yet to be overcome on both sides. For instance, corporates sometimes feel that NGOs are not well governed, that they do not have systems and processes in place, that they are not sufficiently outcome- or impact-oriented. On the other hand, NGOs feel that corporates in their role of funders are highhanded and do not have an understanding of development processes or community realties, yet want to dictate how CSR projects are to be carried out, and that they do not respect development sector work as professional work.

The reality is that these are two different worlds, and there has to be a conscious and sustained effort on both sides to build trust and mutual respect. There needs to be an acceptance of the fact that each has much to learn from the other. Corporates cannot treat NGOs as subcontractors. They have to respect the professional expertise that they bring, the commitment that they have, and their understanding of communities. The NGOs have to appreciate that corporates work with a different mindset, have different compulsions, and are used to different types of timelines, deadlines, as well as different governance and management systems.

When there is a sincere effort to build a collaborative partnership, there is an opportunity for both sides to learn and change. For instance, a corporate can definitely benefit from interaction with expert NGOs to learn about social and environmental concerns and how it (the corporate) can be part of the solution; or how it may be part of the problem without knowing it! Corporates need to see their implementing partners as bridges to better understand community and social development, while NGOs can benefit from adapting and adopting systems and processes used in the corporate. Such CSR partnerships are in fact a great opportunity for two different worlds to come together.

An NGO working with a corporate should not only be looking to financial grants to enable it to carry out projects but must also realize that non-financial partnerships can be very valuable too—for instance, if a corporate can help them set up an MIS system, or improve their accounting and financial processes, etc. On the other hand, corporates can look to NGOs to help them with ensuring that environmental and social sensitivities are built into their business planning.

Corporates who have been working with NGOs and have mature CSR partnerships recognize this. They move towards a mode of co-creation of CSR projects seeing their implementing partners as extensions of the corporate's own capacity, and recognize that these are partnerships, not transactions. They put in place systems to help partnerships succeed. Some best practices adopted by corporates include capacity-building workshops to help NGOs understand the requirements of the CSR law; process familiarization workshops for new partners where they share the overall CSR vision and strategy; annual partnership meets which are a platform for all their NGO partners; helping partners set up their systems, processes, etc. Understanding the constraints of the partners, they develop reporting systems which ease the burden of the NGO while giving the corporate the information it needs, when it needs it.

A critical aspect in funding NGOs and implementing partners is the issue of administrative and staff costs. Very often, corporates are ready to pay for programmatic costs, but not overheads. NGOs today have few sources of income and it is difficult for them to sustain without this support. While it may seem to make sense for a corporate to beat down these costs, it ultimately weakens the NGO, the non-profit ecosystem, and the impacts they are able to deliver. NGOs too need to attract good staff, put into place strong systems and processes, spend time on strategy development, provide proper infrastructure, and be sustainable. The 'Pay What It Takes' movement initiated by the Bridgespan Group and other philanthropists in India is a step towards addressing this chronic problem of underfunding of NGOs.

The ecosystem of this relationship is developing, and should surely see maturation in the near future.

Selection of Evaluation Agencies

The law mandates external evaluations for certain size of projects. Rigorous external scrutiny gives valuable feedback and also helps enhance credibility with various stakeholders. Such evaluation reports are now often a part of assessments for significant awards.

Many corporates may already have a process in place to evaluate entire programmes or large thematic areas or geographies of the programme, at specific intervals—say once in five years. However, selection of agencies for evaluation of programmes is in itself a challenging task.

Management consultancy firms, both large and small, as well as audit firms, now have wings which undertake such evaluations. Then there are large, well-established NGOs as well as specialist firms and individuals with expertise in evaluation who could undertake these assignments. Yet another possibility is to engage academic institutions. The law now permits international agencies also to undertake evaluations. In the scenario when evaluation is mandated, there is a sharp increase in the number of organizations offering such services. For an evaluation to be credible, the agency carrying it out has to be credible. Hence it is critical to evaluate the evaluator before one hands over the evaluation to them!

But it is not a big name which guarantees credibility. The process of the evaluation of evaluators should focus on ensuring that some of the frequently encountered challenges are avoided. These challenges may include:

Shortage of relevant capacity in the Agency

Sometimes consulting entities do not allocate sufficiently senior resources for the exercise as these are not very large-ticket projects, and this can cause a lot of heartburn at later stages. Moreover, they may not have many people who are social development specialists, and therefore may be deploying persons lacking relevant exposure and experience. Since social development is sometimes not seen as a separate professional discipline, the assumption is that the same metrics and measures as used for business evaluations can be deployed here too. Not only in terms of metrics, the mindset with which the evalution of a social development project must be approached is different from evaluating business-related processes.

A very real issue is that while the initial presentations are often made by senior and mid-level staff, they may not have time to devote for later stages. It is understandable that senior people will not do the fieldwork, data compilation or initial drafting. But they need to spend enough time on the research design, on selecting the right team, briefing those doing fieldwork, analysing the data and drawing the conclusions. Inexperienced people going into the field and talking to stakeholders has been known at times to cause problems for the corporate or the implementing agency. Similarly, not understanding social development leads to less-than-fair comments on the processes and outcomes; not understanding the context sometimes leads to impractical recommendations. The issue of senior people not being allocated may be a problem even when large NGOs take up this task.

Bias

Biases cannot be ruled out of these evaluations. For instance, when an NGO is doing the evaluation, it will come with its own perceptions of CSR and corporates (which may sometimes be negative). This does colour the judgements. Also, NGOs may not be able to appreciate the constraints and challenges of CSR vis-à-vis NGO work. This again may lead them to think from a frame of 'I would have done this' or 'I would have done it like this'.

Delays and time slippages

Whichever be the type of entity, delays often happen for a variety of reasons. Other larger projects may take precedence. It may be difficult for the agency to deploy enough people for fieldwork. Or the field areas may be remote. In case academic organizations are involved, educational timetables and schedules may take precedence over such projects.

Too compliant or too rigid

A healthy evaluation process involves two-way communication. When the evaluator has understood the programme and scope, and then visits the field and collects and analyses the data, he sees a certain picture. It is necessary to share this picture with the implementers and managers to understand better if there is some distortion, and more importantly, what the reasons are for things being the way they are. The final report has to evolve from these discussions, and be seen to be fair by both the evaluator and the implementer. It is not unknown for implementing agencies or CSR managers to want to push through certain recommendations or keep certain information close to their chest. Equally, it is not unknown for evaluators to give comments and recommendations which may be based on incomplete information or understanding. A good evaluation agency must have a senior person to take these calls with adequate maturity. He/she must neither be pushed by the CSR team nor by the company to give a certain kind of report, nor be closed to suggestions based on proper rationale and logic.

Mitigating the Problem

Many of these problems can be mitigated if adequate time is spent in drawing up the terms of reference by the CSR team concerned or the corporate. Apart from clarity on what the evaluation will cover, the research methodology, timelines, periodic reviews and interactions as part of the process, would all need to be spelt out to avoid heartburn at later stages.

Scope of evaluation

An evaluation could look at the following:

- Is there a well-articulated mission/vision for the CSR and how do the various programmes contribute to this?
- How material are the CSR initiatives? How strategic are they and how do they contribute to risk mitigation and sync with the overall brand image?
- What are the expected outcomes of specific programmes, and how do they measure up to the goals and objectives? What is the impact? (The log frame and theory of change for the initiative could be the basis for this).
- Gathering feedback from key stakeholders.
- Gathering views and perspectives of the senior management
- Evaluation of efficiency and efficacy of the programme against benchmarks.
- Are the programmes sustainable, and are efforts being made to build in sustainability? Are they scalable and what efforts are being made in this direction?

- How do the CSR initiatives, outcomes, systems, and processes measure up vis-à-vis other companies and 'competitors'?
- Identifying best practices, success stories, as well as areas for improvement.
- Evaluating the capacity-building needs of the team.
- Gathering suggestions on how to address the issues thrown up and improve performance and programme outcomes.

Overall, with regard to selection of agencies for both implementation and evaluation, a few steps can help towards better interactions and getting desired results. These include:

- Spending time and effort on framing the terms of reference or memorandum of understanding,
- Checking with peers about their experiences with the agencies,
- Seeing samples of their work, and
- Interaction and discussion between teams to come to an agreed-upon commonality of understanding and approach.

Talking About Your CSR

Many corporates struggle with whether to, and if so how and how much publicity to give their CSR. Even if there is significant and serious CSR being done by the company, overexposure can lead to its being perceived as greenwash or whitewash or window dressing, by both stakeholders and the general public. At the same time, it is important to communicate the good work being done—not only for strategic business reasons but also to open up opportunities for partnerships, share good practices, and to inspire others. While such dissemination is important, companies must use it with caution, with the realization that publicity is a double-edged sword and that a golden mean has to be struck.

Some routes for CSR communication are mandated, like the CSR section in the company's annual report and website, etc. However, these are more in the form of business communications, and they do not reach the general public. Nor do they provide much room for emotion and real-life change stories, which are the most effective ways to communicate CSR initiatives. Hence other media and means are needed.

Developing a communications policy around CSR—either as a part of the overall corporate communications and social media policy or as a stand-alone policy—may be the right place to begin. The policymaking process itself will clarify why (if at all) the top management wants publicity on CSR, and this could then help to answer the other questions. The policy would need to address such questions as:

- Why does the company want to publicize its CSR?
- Who are the primary target audiences?
- Should the effort be to gain frequent coverage, or only coverage for significant milestones?
- Should the coverage be through press releases, or feature articles, or interviews of top management?
- What about paid publicity? Will the company give paid advertisements or publicity about their CSR? (Not from the CSR budget of course!)
- Is the objective to be covered in national media, or in local and regional media?
- Which single medium—print, television, social—will suit the coverage the best, or should it be mixed-media coverage?
- Who pays? Which department will own the media spend—communications, CSR (with the caution that it cannot be

counted against the mandatory expenditure), marketing, or any others?

- What is the coordination process between the communications and CSR departments to be? Who will be the final decision maker? Who will be the CSR spokespersons?

While press and media are important, other ways to share information about the company's CSR efforts need to be explored. The corporate website is a powerful medium. Going beyond the requirements of law on CSR reporting, human interest stories and highlighting the social development initiatives on the company website are good ways to communicate a company's values. Participation in seminars and conferences, as well as academic forums, is another way to reach out to serious audiences.

Getting influencers and opinion makers to visit CSR activity sites and convince themselves first-hand of the genuineness of the effort is an extremely good way to make an impact. Such opinion makers may span a wide range—from community leaders and politicians to bureaucrats and academics, to social development experts and activists.

Another innovative way to get the good word out would be to have various stakeholders, including students from around project areas, to visit or be involved with the ongoing projects.

A company would usually have films and brochures on its CSR as part of its communications repertoire. But it is equally important that the overall company communications—e.g., company brochure, film, and website—reflect the CSR initiatives. This would demonstrate that CSR is integrated into the company's DNA, and is not an add-on.

There needs to be equal focus on internal communication on CSR within the company and even reaching out to employees' families. Knowing what and how much their company is doing is a matter of pride and motivation. It is also a reminder and incentive to be part of the social initiatives of the company. So CSR must also be a part of regular internal communications, and highlighted in town halls, senior management communications, newsletters, etc.

10

The CSR Ecosystem

India has a rich and vibrant culture of development initiatives, CSR, and philanthropy. With increasing interest in corporate and individual spending on social development initiatives, many specialized organizations, networks, and forums have come up to support these activities. Here is a brief look at some major support systems.

The government has set up some specialized institutions in this sector, the including:

Indian Institute of Corporate Affairs (IICA)

The IICA was set up by the Ministry of Corporate Affairs for training and building capacity on various aspects pertaining to corporate regulation and governance, including environmental and social responsibility. The National Foundation for Corporate Social Responsibility (NFCSR) is an apex national institution housed at IICA. It aims to 'build SMART (specific, measurable, achievable, results-focused, and time-bound) CSR ecosystem' (iica.nic.in). One of its objectives is to create a climate where the corporate sector can work synergistically with the government and NGOs. The NFCSR focuses on every aspect of the CSR life cycle, to help companies comply with CSR-related rules and requirements. It extends services including policy advocacy, research and assessments, and real-time monitoring of CSR projects. It plays a significant role in building capacity in this area through certificate programmes in CSR as well as tailor-made training. Through these initiatives, NFCSR plays a lead role in CSR in the country.

National Corporate Social Responsibility (NCSR) Hub

In 2010, Department of Public Enterprises (DPE) issued guidelines for PSUs on CSR. To support the public sector in these endeavours, an NCSR Hub was set up at the Tata Institute of Social Sciences (TISS), Mumbai, with the following responsibilities:

- Nationwide compilation, documentation, and creation of database,
- Advocacy and research,
- Preparation of panels of implementing organizations/ monitoring and valuation agencies,
- Promotional activities, including production of short films, printing of brochures, pamphlets etc.,
- Organizing conferences, seminars, workshops—both national and international,
- Acting as a think tank, and
- Any other matter as entrusted to it from time to time by the DPE (www.tiss.edu).

Centre for CSR, Public Private Partnership and Peoples Action: National Institute of Rural Development (NIRD) and Panchayati Raj

This Centre is housed at NIRD, Hyderabad, and its mandate includes:

- Guiding corporates and other stakeholders, viz., government departments, NGOs, cooperative societies, public and private sector enterprises on CSR initiatives to play a vital role towards sustainable rural development;
- Imparting managerial skills and building capacity on effective public private partnerships (PPP) in rural development;
- Providing a wide range of academic services in the form of specific CSR training programmes on consultancy basis; and
- Undertaking action-oriented research projects, nationwide policy research studies and evaluations on CSR spending and PPP initiatives in the country (nirdpr.org.in).

Information Resources

The Ministry of Corporate Affairs has set up the National CSR Data Portal (csr.gov.in) with the objective to share CSR-related information and data. It has a large amount of data regarding CSR spends across states and sectors, as well as year-wise details of activities and spends of individual companies. It also covers CSR legislation and the CSR awards, and has a brief background of CSR in India. It is the site for official and authentic information with regard to mandatory CSR, and will help stakeholders access fairly updated information and data.

The recently inaugurated National CSR Exchange Portal (https://csrxchange.gov.in/) of the Ministry of Corporate Affairs aims to be an e-platform to help corporates and implementing Agencies to strategize, implement and manage their CSR projects and work effectively towards social development.

Some states have portals or sites dedicated to CSR within the state, which give details with regard to projects, partnerships, and priorities. While some states try to nudge and encourage CSR spends going into certain specific projects, geographical regions, or thrust areas, others have made it mandatory for companies operating in the state and having mandatory CSR requirements, to register on the portal and upload their activities and plans, or seek permissions. On the other hand, some states do not have dedicated CSR sites, but do refer to CSR in their industry-related or other department sites.

The Role of Industry Associations and Professional Bodies in CSR

Industry associations at national, state, or regional levels, have been active in CSR and related subjects for long now. They play many roles—bringing together companies for information sharing and synergy, developing guidelines, documenting CSR efforts, acting as the bridge between industries and the government by playing an advocacy role, and encouraging good efforts through awards and recognitions. Some industry associations themselves take up certain CSR projects.

ASSOCHAM (Associated Chambers of Commerce and Industry of India) has a Committee on Corporate Affairs, Company Law, Corporate Governance and CSR, as well as committees on education, women empowerment, etc. The CII (Confederation of Indian Industry), has initiatives and forums on CSR and community development, disaster management, education, environment, public health, skill development, etc. The FICCI (Federation of Indian Chambers of Commerce and Industry) has committees on CSR and community development, as well as on skill development, agriculture, art and culture, higher education, the FICCI Alliance for Re-Imagining School Education (FICCI ARISE), etc. The PHDCCI (Punjab, Haryana and Delhi Chamber of Commerce and Industry) is also active in convening forums to bring together industries around these topics.

The NASSCOM Foundation which is the social arm of the National Association of Software and Service Companies (NASSCOM), the IT-BPM (Information Technology–Business Process Management) industry body, provides a platform for this industry to bring about social transformation and impact through technology. From industry advocacy and consulting support for CSR law implementation to awards to help foster technology for social good—it takes up a number of initiatives to support its members.

It would be useful for a company to touch base with the local office of any of these bodies. They usually have local committees related to CSR, and are also able to help with networking with other corporates with similar missions.

Today, chartered accountants and company secretaries have a significant role to play in handling CSR, given the legal requirements of interpreting and overseeing the application of rules. The Institute of Chartered Accountants of India (ICAI) has an active CSR Committee which works to improve understanding and compliance of regulations. It undertakes advocacy, projects, training, gives awards, and has also brought out actionable CSR-related guidelines for its members. The Institute of Company Secretaries (ICS) also undertakes training and gives awards. Both ICAI and ICS issue professional guidance to members from time to time, and support industry to undertake advocacy. Other professional associations like the National HRD Network (NHRDN) are also placing an increasing emphasis on CSR as it relates to their professions. These are forums which would help professionals within companies to keep track of developments in their specialized areas.

A critical role of such bodies is to bring together industry concerns, challenges, and perspectives, and represent them to the government. For instance, whenever any changes in CSR Rules are proposed, the government ministries concerned put these up for comments. Bodies such as ASSOCHAM, CII, and FICCI usually ask members for inputs, which they consolidate and present to the government. More proactively, they may also call for discussions among members on specific or emerging challenges, and then make recommendations. They often convene forums where relevant governmental bodies or departments can come together with corporates for discussions on issues of common interest.

Specialized Agencies

The ecosystem, in terms of support agencies and networks for CSR, has also evolved rapidly. Significant examples include the following.

CSRBox

A knowledge and impact-intelligence driven partnerships platform for the development community, CSRBox supports donors and corporates looking to invest in impactful and sustainable projects to find appropriate partners, while also helping implementing agencies to find projects. It aims to drive collaborations and partnerships for positive social impacts. It brings out well-researched reports on CSR-related topics.

Goodera

The platform supports corporates to automate all steps of their CSR life cycle, from grant management process, collecting ground-level data in real time, and tracking impact at beneficiary level. It also helps NGOs to connect with corporates for their CSR and volunteering initiatives. In addition, it has a resource hub for supporting knowledge sharing and learning.

India CSR

This is an information and knowledge hub for CSR in India, and supports networking at a national level. It highlights and encourages CSR, sustainability, and responsible business through highlighting impact stories.

iVolunteer

This NGO works to connect volunteers with organizations that seek to deliver impact in various development sectors. Recognized as one of the country's leading organizations promoting and supporting volunteerism, it currently has over 17,000 volunteers and 300 NGOs in its network. It has taken a lead in recognizing volunteering through the iVolunteer awards.

National CSR Network (NCN)

An initiative of Strategic CSR Alliance, the NCN comprises a panel of professionals from industry to assist companies in India to fulfil their CSR quotient and facilitate implementation of meaningful social and environmental development projects. It provides a platform to share and learn best CSR practices, as also services to individual companies.

Samhita

A CSR consulting firm that works with corporates towards developing impactful CSR initiatives, its effort is to co-create a CSR eco-system of multi-stakeholder partnerships. It offers strategic consulting, research, programme design and management, impact assessment and capacity building. Samhita's Collective Good Foundation identifies and forms partnerships.

Sattva Consulting

This organization is focused on helping 'corporations, philanthropists, foundations and non-profits—succeed in achieving their social impact goals.' Not only do they offer advisory services and help organizations tailor impact social solutions, but also undertake research and analysis in related topics, including CSR. Their 'IndiaDataInsights' site is a rich source of data.

Standards and Certifications for CSR

Standards and certifications from the Geneva-based International Organization for Standardization (ISO) for different activities help to give assurance on processes and systems. Coming to the question of whether there are such standards for CSR, we are once again reminded that nothing about CSR is simple! While there is an ISO standard related to CSR, it is a guidance standard and not a certifiable one.

ISO 26000

This standard was launched globally in 2000, and was adopted in India in 2019. However, it is not a certifiable standard. Rather, it helps 'those who recognize that respect for society and environment is a critical success factor' to clarify and articulate what social responsibility is, and then to turn this understanding into action. It is also a means of learning and sharing best practices. It is generic and can be used by companies of any size, irrespective of sector, size, or geography. In fact, even NGOs and other organizations will find it useful, as it is essentially a tool to ensure a systematic approach to social sector activities.

With organizational governance at the centre, ISO 26000 looks at the following subjects: community involvement and development, human rights, labour practices, environment, fair operating practices, and consumer issues. The standard stresses on respect for stakeholder interests, a holistic approach, practising these principles consciously while keeping in mind interdependencies, and ensuring materiality—i.e., focusing on those subjects which are material to the particular business. While there is no requirement that a company should adopt the standard for their CSR, it is something that can help organizations to plan and implement their CSR activities systematically and in an impactful way (https://www.iso.org/).

While ISO 26000, which is the specific CSR standard, may not be certifiable, there are some related standards which may be used for specific CSR-related activities. For instance, many companies run educational institutions or offer healthcare under their CSR. There are ISO standards which can be used for such specific sectors, including the following:

ISO 21001

This looks at management systems for educational organizations, to help them showcase 'their ability to support the acquisition and development of competence through teaching, learning or research'.

ISO 9000

This is often used to ensure standardized levels of quality across different aspects of healthcare, from hospitals and long-term care facilities to pharmaceutical companies.

ISO 9001

This is another useful standard which is a generic, certifiable standard that provides quality management assurance of an organization. Increasingly, NGOs and non-profits are choosing to be certified under this, to both improve their internal processes and also increase credibility with donors and other external stakeholders. ISO 9001 is based on certain principles including 'a strong customer focus, the motivation and implication of top management, the process approach and continual improvement'.

At the core is the use of the process approach. That means setting out the organization's work as a set of interrelated and interacting activities performed in a systematic way. If an organization wants to improve performance, it must identify the weak points in one or more processes and improve them. The use of the approach can help non-profit organizations put systems and processes in place, and contribute to gaining greater confidence with stakeholders.

ISO 14001

This standard sets out the criteria for an environmental management system and can be certified. In the context of CSR, if a company is undertaking significant environment-related programmes, it can provide assurance to the company and external stakeholders that environmental impact is being measured and improved.

ISO 20400

This is a recent standard for sustainable procurement. It provides guidance for organizations of any size or type to ensure sustainable outcomes through their supply chains through a strategic framework for sustainable procurement.

Apart from ISO, there are of course sector-specific accreditations and certifications for specific institutions which will help ensure quality, e.g., National Accreditation Board for Hospitals and Healthcare Providers (NABH) for hospitals; accreditation with National Skill Development Corporation (NSDC) schemes for vocational training centres, etc.

Technology for CSR

As in everything else, technology has an increasing role to play in the development sector and CSR. There is the category of technology tools which can help bring in efficiencies in CSR management—for instance, end-to-end technology-enabled solutions for CSR project-cycle management, or for tracking outcomes, outputs, and impacts.

Telemedicine, simulation tools for technical training, and remote-education are other tools that have helped CSR programmes pivot during Covid, and these changes are here to stay. Several technology tools can aid CSR programmes—from handheld devices which help to update health status of children in remote villages into a central database, or tracking soil health, or AI technology to estimate groundwater.

It has now become necessary for CSR managers to keep track of relevant developments to be able to deploy them effectively. With of course the caveat that there is also a lot of hard sell in the space as well as gimmicky products, and a critical evaluation is necessary about which technologies and products can really add value in the long run.

Staffing for Effective CSR

The first and foremost thing when discussing staffing of the CSR function is to recognize that social development is a professional field and that the CSR team or foundation needs to be staffed by specialized professionals. The ecosystem has evolved to support this need. There are now an increasing number of specialized sites like DevNetJobsIndia, CSRBox, GoBarefoot, as well as recruitment agencies like Third Sector Partners, who cater exclusively for this sector. Using these is usually the best way to get a wide selection.

Sometimes companies underestimate the importance of expertise while staffing the CSR department and deploy surplus junior and mid-level staff from other departments to this function. This is a sub-optimal solution which undermines the importance of the function and assumes that it needs no special skills or that mediocrity is acceptable here.

At leadership levels, corporates may deploy senior business leaders who are successful in their domains and would now like to move to CSR, away from the rat race, and with a desire for self-actualization. This sentiment is laudable, and must be respected. However, while a good leader is a good leader irrespective of where he or she is positioned, the move must be done with the recognition that the social sector is fundamentally different from business, in terms of mindset, approach, subject matter, and maybe even ideology, and that the incumbent will have to spend considerable time unlearning and learning before taking a leadership position here.

But before one starts a recruitment process, it would be good to get an overview of what makes a good CSR professional. What does one look for in recruiting junior or mid-level CSR staff? A postgraduation in social work (MSW), development management, or rural development from reputed institutions is a good starting point, though not essential if relevant experience compensates. Some MSW programmes have started offering specialization in CSR, or at least a course on the same. These courses may cover sustainability and CSR. Such an exposure may be relevant when recruiting freshers.

Experience of community-based work, maturity, balance, and negotiation and conflict-resolution skills are critical for a CSR professional. The challenges of CSR in the field require a good deal of stakeholder management, with implications for business operations. Hence, someone with field experience is usually better than a fresher. The ability to balance business needs while keeping community interests in the focus requires maturity and clarity of vision. Expertise or experience in the relevant thrust area of interest to the company, e.g., education, health, rural development, etc., is of course important.

There are several courses for fresh and working professionals, and such certification is an indication of both domain knowledge and an interest in exploring the field. The NFCSR offers a nine-month certificate course in Strategic CSR. Indira Gandhi National Open University (IGNOU) has come out with different offerings in CSR. HCL Foundation Academy runs several courses, including 'Corporate Social Responsibility: Its Applied Aspects', a three-month, online certificate course. The ICAI has a certificate course. Several other institutions offer courses of varying length and focus: Mudra Institute of Communications has a specialized course on CSR and Communications in partnership with CSRBox; India CSR offers a certificate programme; TISS National CSR Hub organizes tailor-made programmes for PSUs, NGOs, and others. Various NGOs and networks like the National CSR Network and CSRBox offer several short-term programmes.

Today, with CSR having gained some maturity in the country, there is a large pool of people with relevant experience. An important factor to check when recruiting someone who has already worked in CSR, is the match of the CSR philosophy of the candidate's previous organization to that of the recruiting organization. For instance, if the person being considered is from a company which looks at CSR as largely a public relations or corporate relations exercise, it may not suit another company which has a different perspective. Non-government organizations and the non-profit sector are good places to look for possible candidates for CSR jobs. As always, referrals from existing employees, Board and CSR Committee members, and other well-wishers are a good point to start.

It is critical for the CSR team to be closely involved in the entire process of recruitment of CSR professionals. Also, there should be social workers and CSR professionals on the interview panels, besides HR and other managers.

Capacity Building

There are two aspects to capacity building for effective CSR. The first is the sensitization of the business side to a deeper understanding of CSR beyond Section 135—responsible business, good governance, stakeholder orientation, the need for embedding social and environmental concerns into the making of business decisions; and the second is the focus on relevant training for CSR staff, which could span many areas. Assessment and analysis of training needs and other options to build capacity are discussed below.

As mentioned above, the first aspect looks at sensitizing businesses to the larger perspective of social responsibility and community development. As professionals move into business leadership positions, they need to internalize that the social development sector is fundamentally different from the field of business. It cannot be monitored, regulated, and directed as business operations are. It requires developing a deep respect for communities and listening to them; it is about complex change processes which may take decades; it is about continual engagement with a variety of stakeholders.

Senior management needs to understand that India has a rich and deep history of thinking about social transformation and of social development work, and any solutions that may come up within the walls of a CEO's room need to be tested against these. It would be unfair to expect corporate managements to get into the complexities of solutions, but an appreciation of the complexities of the problems is essential. Such an understanding will lead to development of meaningful CSR interventions.

Chief executive officers and senior leaders often do have an understanding of these issues, but middle management may not be equally sensitized. Since they are the ones at the operational level, their orientation is critical. Their understanding and expectations from CSR may often not be fully aligned to even their own company's perspective. They may, for instance, see CSR as an instant solution for a problem with the community, or primarily as a tool for nullifying community opposition or creating a good image. Such a mindset may make it difficult for CSR programmes to be properly implemented. A positive trend is that many MBA programmes are now offering core courses touching topics like sustainability, CSR, governance, ethics, etc., which will help to orient future managers in these perspectives.

It is also important for business-side professionals interfacing with CSR, for example, the company secretary or the chief financial officer, to keep abreast of the CSR Rules and their nuances.

The second aspect of capacity building for CSR is of course of the staff involved in this function. The normal means of training and capacity building that most corporates deploy also apply to CSR. There are several institutions offering training programmes on CSR, but their relevance, duration, effectiveness, and cost-effectiveness need to be examined.

Since CSR provisions and the interpretation of these are changing fast, participation in forums which discuss these is important for senior members of the CSR function. Equally, it is important for them to keep abreast of new developments in the larger space of sustainability, governance, etc. Here are a few useful options.

Short-term programmes on focused areas

Such programmes on areas such as agricultural innovations, water management, innovative pedagogies, low-cost sanitation, etc., as relevant to company CSR are important for field-level staff, to keep up with best practices. Training needs analysis may also throw up specific requirements like understanding log frame development, social return on investment, documentation, monitoring, etc., for which specific people need to be deputed in order that the team as a whole has these skills.

Tailor-made training programmes

This is another option focusing on the specific challenges, opportunities, and thrusts of the company.

Field visits

Visits to peer and related organizations are usually very helpful to CSR staff. All levels of CSR staff would benefit from properly planned field visits, which allow them to understand implementation of initiatives, as well as provide opportunity for interactions with their peers, the community and other stakeholders. Equally, having senior social sector and CSR leaders from other organizations visit the company's CSR programmes and having frank discussions on strengths and weaknesses would greatly enrich capacity of staff and enhance the quality of initiatives.

In-house training programmes

A range of general and management skills are required for the CSR arm, as they are for any unit of the business. In case of such generic skills, a good option is for the CSR team to take advantage of the overall corporate training initiatives. For instance, if the CSR team members need to strengthen their general management, project management, or communication skills, it may be useful to join the company's training programmes in these subjects.

The generic principles may then be adapted to the specific context of the social development initiatives. Moreover, such joint exercises help the CSR team integrate better with other parts of the corporate. The CSR team needs to understand their company's business and keep itself updated with developments in this regard. Such business orientation needs to be organized at regular intervals.

There is no dearth of innovations and best practices in social development and CSR sectors. Often however, these are not known beyond the organization and its partners. It is always useful for professionals to keep up with these. Even if they are not replicable, they may be adaptable.

Attending seminars, conferences and webinars

There are plenty of such events and in fact one must be choosy in this regard, ensuring one spends time and resources in picking the most relevant and useful ones. These events are also obviously useful networking opportunities.

Studying the CSR of leaders

Today, every company or foundation's website has detailed descriptions of the initiatives, often including process documentation, so that one can understand not just what was done, but also how. It would be especially interesting to study the practices of the best. Platforms like CSRBox showcase such best practices.

Signing up for newsletters

Many foundations and trusts have their own newsletter. It is a matter of a few clicks to sign on. There are also thematic newsletters brought out by specialized institutions, and these are useful for technical knowledge.

Research reports, compilations, yearbooks, etc.

Industry associations as well as independent organizations bring out compilations and edited volumes of the efforts of various companies and foundations in the area of CSR or on specific thematic areas. These are useful documents.

An important point to bear in mind is that the legislation allows a company to deploy funds to build capacity of company staff for CSR, but this has to be fitted within the overall 5 per cent administrative spend limit!

Awards and Recognitions for CSR

Applying for any award is a very useful exercise, in that it forces organizations to document their practices and focus on outcomes. It is an opportunity to sit back and reflect; to get the perspectives of objective outsiders; and to benchmark against the best. Often it is an opportunity for internal dialogue within the organization, as many departments and many levels are involved in creating a strong application. And it is also an opportunity for creating internal pride and to bring external recognition.

Of course, to fulfil these objectives, the award needs to be reputed and the process to be fair and thorough. Over the last few years, there has been a proliferation of awards. Before a company sends in its application to be considered for an award, it is important to ensure that the award is worth applying for, that it is not something that can be bought, say with a sponsorship towards the awards function. Getting less-than-reputed awards may in fact reduce the seriousness with which the CSR efforts of a company are seen.

There are awards for CSR; sectoral awards like Best/Most Innovative Practices in Health or Education or Skilling, etc.; awards for companies for their CSR programmes; and awards for foundations for implementing CSR effectively. With the focus on overall business responsibility and Section 135, now there are more awards for companies, rather than for implementing agencies.

Whenever a call for applications is received, it makes sense for a company seeking to apply for the award to first check out the website of the organizers, look into the nature of the organization giving the award, the people behind it, the age of the organization, its other activities, etc., and also who the previous winners of the awards have been. This will help to gauge how seriously the award should be taken.

Some of the things to check before applying for an award would include the following;

Credibility of the organization offering the award

The most coveted awards in the stable are probably the CSR awards of the Ministry of Corporate Affairs. They are backed by the credibility of the government, and are awarded after a very detailed and rigorous process worked out by eminent people.

Some other notable awards include The Golden Peacock award instituted by the Institute of Directors (IOD) India, and those instititutEd by industry bodies like the ASSOCHAM, the CII, the FICCI, and the PHDCCI. Independent bodies like CSRBox also give awards which are respected. Sectoral or state-level industry bodies also give away awards.

Credibility of the process

The thoroughness of the process is what makes an award worth applying for. Good awards usually involve a multistage process, with submission of documents including evaluation reports, followed by field visits, ground-truthing and verification as integral processes. Some may also involve discussions with CEOs and senior management, as well as external stakeholders, apart from the CSR teams. Such tiered steps, starting with a paper application, and going on to more in-depth interactions, are indicators of a strong process. Often, shortlisting processes are outsourced to reputed audit or consultancy firms or well-known NGOs, which brings in standardization. Some awards insist on nomination through an industry body, professional institution, etc., which is another check on the applicants.

Nature of award

A typical red flag is too many categories of awards. If there are logical and limited categories, say, based on size of company or sector of industry, it makes sense. But too many categories may be simply a way of giving away a larger number of awards and pleasing more people.

Credibility of the people involved

The final selection is usually done by a jury. Needless to say, the credibility and standing of the jury is a reflection of the credibility of the award.

The fees

A thorough process involves costs—the time spent by people at different stages, travel costs for field visits, communication costs, administrative costs, etc. Hence many awards do have an application fee. The issue here is to discern whether it is a reasonable fee, or whether it looks like a money making gambit, or even payment to buy the award!

One key link missing in even the best award processes today is a feedback loop. The awarding institutions seldom revert to organizations that do not make the cut, to tell them what could be improved. If this could be added to the process of award application, the experience would be even more enriching for all involved.

Once the decision has been taken to apply for an award, the involvement of the senior management is critical. Since many awards require information not only related to the CSR angle but also on financials, governance practices, HR and ethics policies, environmental initiatives, etc., it is an internal exercise involving many departments. This is best managed through an effort coordinated at a senior level.

A mature CSR programme should hold itself up for awards scrutiny and see this as a benchmarking process. Whether it wins or loses, it will be a learning-and-networking experience.

Box 10.1: National Corporate Social Responsibility (CSR) Awards by Ministry of Corporate Affairs

The Ministry of Corporate Affairs instituted National Corporate Social Responsibility Awards to recognize companies that have made a positive impact on the society through their innovative and sustainable CSR initiatives.

The Awards seek to:

- Encourage companies to spend the entire amount, i.e., eligible CSR spend;
- Recognize the impact, innovation, usage of technology, gender and environment issues, sustainability, scalability, and replicability of CSR activities; and
- Channelize CSR activities of corporates so that the benefits of their activities reach the marginalized sections of society and in remote areas of the country

https://iica.nic.in/nacsr.aspx

So here is wishing your CSR initiatives the very best. May they win many awards, and more importantly, may they be done right, done for the right reasons, done in the right spirit, and may they make a difference!

Annexure 1

Sample Corporate Social Responsibility Policy
XXX Pvt. LTD

Introduction

XXX Pvt. Ltd (herein after refered to as the company) has developed a CSR policy in alignment with its objective and values, as a blueprint to achieve its goal to be a socially and environmentally responsible corporate citizen. The policy defines the principles and mechanisms for CSR programmes in accordance with Section 135 of the Companies Act, 2013.

It is applicable to all the CSR activities of the company.

The Board may, from time to time, modify the CSR policy as suitable.

VISION

The CSR thrust of the company shall be to bring about sustainable enhancement in the quality of life of the communities around its plants, offices, and operations, through community-based, participatory programmes involving women, youth, farmers, and other vulnerable groups. It shall also contribute to disasters and other such causes in times of need.

It shall contribute in measurable ways to the relevant SDGs. The CSR programmes will be part of the ESG thrust of the company.

The CSR initiatives will also be a means for the company's employees and their families to become involved in social development.

CSR FOCUS AREAS

The core areas of interventions and activities shall be:

- Education (within the gamut of Schedule VII, promoting education, including special education and employment-enhancing vocational skills especially among children, women, elderly, and the differently abled, and livelihood enhancement projects): The company shall take up educational activities, with a special focus on providing skill training to unemployed youth.
- Empowering Women (within the gamut of promoting gender equality, empowering women, setting up homes and hostels for women and orphans; setting up old age homes, daycare centres and such other facilities for senior citizens, and measures for reducing inequalities faced by socially and economically backward groups): This shall be through supporting women self-help groups for capacity building, livelihoods development, and individual and group enterprises.

- Rural Development: With special focus on farmers, their capacity building, and various types of interventions to improve their incomes and livelihoods.
- Eradicating Hunger, Poverty, and Malnutrition: These initiatives will specially focus on preventing malnutrition in children and adolescents.
- Response to Humanitarian Disasters: The company may, from time to time, take up any activities in response to disasters either in its communities or anywhere else in the country as needed.

Geography of Initiatives

The company shall undertake most of its activities around various areas of its operations, including areas of proposed operations.

In case of emergencies, disasters, or humanitarian crisis, the Board shall, after due deliberation, allocate resources to causes of local or national importance, outside of these areas.

The company shall ensure that no activities under the following heads are counted as CSR:

a) Activities that benefit only the employees of the company and their families.
b) Contributions of any amount directly or indirectly to any political party under Section 182 of the Companies Act, 2013.
c) One-off events such as marathons/ awards/ charitable contribution/ advertisement/ sponsorships of TV programmes, etc.
d) Expenses incurred by the company for the fulfilment of any other Act/statute or regulations (such as labour laws, Land Acquisition Act, etc.)

CSR Budget

- The Board shall ensure that in each financial year, the company spends at least 2 per cent of the average net profit made during the three immediately preceding financial years on CSR activities.
- The computation of average net profits shall be carried out in accordance with the provisions of Section 198 of the Companies Act, 2013.
- The budgets shall be built ground-up and the Board shall consider and provide adequate resources for essential activities even if the profits are inadequate for meeting the needs.
- While the effort will be to ensure that there is no unutilized budget, in case there should be, this will be treated as per the law prevalent at the time.
- Surplus arising, if any, out of any CSR projects/ programmes/ activities, shall not form part of the business profit of the company.

Implementation

- The mode of implementation of CSR programmes will be a combination of implementation through the company foundation, its own CSR foundation set up for the purpose of undertaking CSR, and through partners such as NGOs, registered societies, etc., meeting the requirements of the law and selected after due diligence.
- The company or the company foundation may enter into partnerships with the government, business partners, and communities to create multiplier effect of its social and environment projects.

- They may collaborate or pool resources with other organizations (its subsidiary companies and NGOs) to plan, implement, monitor, and report CSR activities.
- Services of internal teams, expert agencies, consultancy firms, etc., may be used wherever required for carrying out baseline surveys, guidance on project design and implementation, due diligence of implementation partners, impact assessment, etc.
- Each initiative will have clear objectives, plans, timelines, outcomes, indicators, and budgets; and progress will be monitored on a biannual basis by the CSR Committee.
- The company shall encourage employees for volunteering in community service.

Oversight

- The CSR Committee shall monitor the progress of activities twice a year, and present the same to the Board.
- The company shall ensure impact assessments as per the law, and also encourage internal or external evaluations of significant initiatives from time to time, for feedback and any improvements and course corrections.

Reporting

- The Board shall ensure to meet the requirements of communication and reporting as per the law.

Programme Details for the Year ...

Computation of mandatory CSR spend at 2 per cent of the average net profit made during the three immediately preceding financial years in accordance with Section 198: Rs ...

CSR Project	Relevance As Per Schedule VII	Mode of Implementation	Where	Outcomes	Timeline	Budget	Monitoring Process
Support to improve educational achievement in students in government schools	Promoting Education	Through XXX Foundation	AAA, BBB, CCC villages in district 111, State 222	At least 500 students in standards 6 to 8 in these schools are provided after-school support, study material, e-classes, etc.	From June to March	Rs---	Pre-intervention assessment of academic level, mid-term and final assessments. Attendance records.

CSR Project	Relevance As Per Schedule VII	Mode of Implementation	Where	Outcomes	Timeline	Budget	Monitoring Process
Supporting women self-help groups for income generation projects	Promoting gender equality, empowering women	Through partner NGO YYY	AAA, BBB, CCC villages in district 111, State 222	At least six new enterprises created and functional. Business takes off.	From April to March	Rs ---	Sixty women involved actively. Bank accounts operated. Operationally self-sufficient in three months.
Administration						Rs ---	5 per cent of total CSR budget
TOTAL							

Annexure 2

Sample Preliminary Needs Assessment And Baseline Report

Baseline survey and Needs Analysis was undertaken in proposed project villages. The design of the baseline format was developed based on the three broad areas of interventions: Education, Health, and Livelihood. Baseline household survey was conducted for 390 households.

Village-level information collected from local government sources indicates the following facts:

A. Land information:

#	Information	Village A	Village B	Village C	Total
a.	Area of the village (in hectares)	845	311	269	1425

#	Information	Village A	Village B	Village C	Total
b.	Total forest land and area (ha)	25	0	0	25
c.	Number of government canals	1	0	0	1
d.	Number of wells (with electricity)	388	180	106	674
e.	Number of tube wells (with electricity)	100	0	0	100
f.	Number of tanks	6	0	0	6
g.	Number of seasonal Streams	10	12	7	29
h.	Others—natural sprigs	1	0	0	1
i.	Total irrigated area (ha)	397	192	176	765
j.	Un-irrigated area (ha)	197	46	28	271

#	Information	Village A	Village B	Village C	Total
k.	Culturable waste (including gauchar and groves) (ha)	183	50	40	273
l.	Area not available for cultivation (ha)	68	23	25	116

B. General Information of villages:

- Total number of houses in the villages are 941 (468 in A, 313 in B and 160 in C).
- Total number of hamlets in these villages are twelve.
- Total 4,325 people reside in these villages out of which 2,352 are male and 1,973 are female. A total of total 24.09 per cent population belongs to the Schedule Castes. There is no Scheduled Tribes population.
- The total population of children in age group of 0–3 years, 4–5 years, and 6–14 years is given below:

Age group	Male	Female	Total
Children 0–3 years	172	152	324
Children 4–5 years	131	127	258
Children 6–14 years	288	251	539
Total disabled	16	9	25

C. Educational Facilities:

#	Information		Village A	Village B	Village C	Total
a.	Number of primary schools		4	1	1	6
b.	Number of middle schools		1	1	0	2
c.	Number of secondary (high) schools		1	0	0	1
d.	College and inter colleges are available within range (km)		16	16	16	
e.	Number of children going to Anganwadi		111	64	72	247
f.	Number of children admitted to primary school	Male	32	13	8	53
g.	Number of children admitted to primary school	Female	24	8	6	38
h.	Number of children retain /regular in primary school	Male	144	62	35	241

#	Information		Village A	Village B	Village C	Total
i.	Number of children retain /regular in primary school	Female	149	69	25	243
j.	Number of children admitted to middle school	Male	31	15	3	49
k.	Number of children admitted to middle school	Female	27	9	0	36
l.	Number of children retain /regular in middle school	Male	114	47	0	161
m.	Number of children retain /regular in middle school	Female	100	36	0	136
n.	Number of children admitted in high school	Male	41	12	0	53
o.	Number of children admitted in high school	Female	32	8	0	40

#	Information		Village A	Village B	Village C	Total
p.	Number of children dropping out after middle school	Male	12	0	0	12
q.	Number of children dropping out after middle school	Female	14	0	0	14
r.	Teacher–student ratio in primary school		29:1	44:1	31:1	
s.	Teacher–student ratio in middle school		214:1	42:1	0	

All the schools in the area have good and well-maintained buildings but no or very poor toilet facilities. There are no teaching materials, kits, science lab materials of any sort in any of the schools. There are two computers in each school, but these do not seem to be in working condition except in Village B. No sports facilities and play materials are available in the schools.

D. Health Facilities

a. There is no government allopathic, Ayurvedic, homeopathic or Unani hospital in the villages. The block-level hospital is located at MMM—the block headquarters, about 16 km from the villages. However, there is a place called NNN about 12 km from the villages which has private nursing homes and doctors.

b. There is only one health sub-centre located in CCC village which is not functional.
c. There are community health workers, village midwives (trained ladies for conducting delivery) and Accredited Social Health Activitists (ASHA) workers appointed by government in all the villages.
d. There is only one Auxiliary Nurse Midwife (ANM) for these villages who visits once in a month to each village. There is no ambulance facility in the area.
e. No infant and mother mortality cases have been reported in the villages in last year and most of the pregnant women are immunized by health worker.
f. There are six Anganwadis. All have taken proactive role in caring of malnourished children (less than ten in the three villages).
g. There are only 312 houses having latrine out of which 289 houses use them.
h. Mosquitoes and flies are a very severe problem causing dengue, malaria and various stomach-related diseases in the villages.
i. Hand pumps (numbering thirty) and open wells (numbering twenty-two) are the main source of drinking water in the villages.
j. Wells provide sufficient water till March but in summer, there is water crisis. The water quality in most of the wells is poor due to contamination and salinity.

E. Other Amenities

a. Out of the three villages, only village A has a post office. Other than this there is no telephone office or telephone connection available in the villages. However, mobile phones are owned and used by almost all the houses.

b. There is no bus service to these villages, only private autos operating.
c. The railway and bus services are available in KKK about 12 km from these villages.
d. There is no bank or cooperatives available in these villages, only one credit society is located in village C which provides credit for agricultural purposes only.
e. There is no recreational and cultural facility available in the villages except Bhajan Mandalis.
f. The approach roads to villages B and C are mud roads.
g. There is power supply available in these villages but electricity supply to village C is disconnected due to non-payment of bills by villagers.
h. No newspaper and magazines reach the villages. However, most households have TV and cable connections.

F. Livelihood Picture

a. Agriculture, livestock, and wage labour including those under government schemes are the main occupations in the villages.
b. Agricultural productivity of cereal crops in the area is very poor compared to state average.
c. The cropping is mostly done in the Rabi season and most of the land remains fallow during the Kharif season. More than 60 per cent Rabi cultivation is irrigated while Kharif cultivation is 100 per cent rainfed.
d. Farmers are not well informed about soil fertility, organic farming, and scientific agriculture.
e. There is no industry in the vicinity of these villages except mining of granite and stone crushing. Villagers go to stone crushing units for wage labour.

f. Other than cultivation, no off-farm product is manufactured in the village and sold out from these villages.
g. There are a few rich farmers in the villages who have tied up with National Seeds Corporation (NSC) and other private seed companies for Rabi seed production.
h. There is one NGO working here, which has initiated SHG programmes. There are fourteen SHGs in the villages out of which four have taken up midday meal preparation as an income generation activity (IGA), and six have taken up small IGAs at individual levels.
i. Out of the total population, 20–25 per cent (numbering 973) are in the age group 19–30. Most of them are educated up to 8th standard. Hardly 20 per cent (195 youths) of the total youth population have completed education up to 12th standard or above. About eight youth have undergone skill training programmes of the government. Out of these one is employed in the nearby town, three have set up their own auto repair shop, while the others are not doing anything. Most of the youth in the villages are not interested in agriculture-related jobs.

Annexure 3

Sample Stakeholder Analysis

Please note: The highlighted portions of the analysis stem from the fact that this is a CSR project rather than a project by an independent development agency or NGO, and this is a factor of the community being a stakeholder in the business.

Sample: Stakeholder Analysis for CSR Skill Training Programmein vicinity of Plant works

Stakeholder	Impact	Influence	Importance For Stakeholder	How S/He Could Contritbute	How S/He Could Hamper	Strategy To Engange Stakeholder
Trainee	High	High	Opportunity for skilling, certification Gaining livelihood	Taking up the opportunity sincerely Taking up job/self employment	Not joining Dropping out Not taking up livelihood opportunity	Proper matching of interest and selection of skill Counselling to help them overcome problems Handholding to support in job/ self employment

Stakeholder	Impact	Influence	Importance For Stakeholder	How S/ He Could Contritbute	How S/ He Could Hamper	Strategy To Engange Stakeholder
					Insistence that after skilling, they be guaranteed employment in the company plant.	Counselling and clear communication before, during and after the course that the skilling will not lead to employment in the plant.

Stakeholder	Impact	Influence	Importance For Stakeholder	How S/ He Could Contritbute	How S/ He Could Hamper	Strategy To Engange Stakeholder
Parents	Medium	Medium	Skill development of their ward Employment will support the family	Encouraging and motivating ward to join the course. Supporting the ward's livelihood initiatives. monitoring of the youth	Parents may prefer sending their children to earn rather than go for skill training May discourage them to go out of their hometowns for jobs.	Home visits Motivation/ awareness programmesto share long term perspective of skilled jobs Parents meetings Family level counselling

Stakeholder	Impact	Influence	Importance For Stakeholder	How S/ He Could Contritbute	How S/ He Could Hamper	Strategy To Engange Stakeholder
Training Manager and Staff	High	High	Identifying the potential youth Helping the youth in selecting the course Constant Monitoring for quality training inputs, successful completion and placement	Motivating trainees Maintaining level of programme quality Customizing programme based on the capabilities of the trainees Providing counselling and handholding as well as proper placement	Not being in touch with trainee aspirations Not having good rapport with employers, youth, faculty, etc.	Ongoing efforts for their capacity building and motivation. Good HR practices.

Stakeholder	Impact	Influence	Importance For Stakeholder	How S/ He Could Contritbute	How S/ He Could Hamper	Strategy To Engange Stakeholder
Managers of Govt. Schemes	High	Medium	Valid certification. Monetary support for organization and the trainees	Clear norms for training institutions and programmes Timely actions in accreditation, approvals, budget releases.	Delays in various processes Individual interpretation of norms, leading to confusion on the ground.	Constant communication Showcasing of facilities and processes to key decision makers Being a part of various forums and sharing ideas for the enhancement of skill ecosystem.

Stakeholder	Impact	Influence	Importance For Stakeholder	How S/ He Could Contritbute	How S/ He Could Hamper	Strategy To Engange Stakeholder
Community leaders and NGOs	Medium	Medium	Helping with mobilization from their communities. Communicating with parents and youth and counselling them.	Knowledge of community in their area can help in mobilization, counselling and building trust. Ground community presence can help in monitoring.	May not be proactive. May expect some quid pro quo. Insistence that after skilling, they be guaranteed employment in the company plant.	Constant communication. Sharing plans and progress transparently. Showcasing the benefits t their community from the interventions. Counselling and clear communication before, during and after the course that the skilling will not lead to employment in the plant.

Stakeholder	Impact	Influence	Importance For Stakeholder	How S/ He Could Contritbute	How S/ He Could Hamper	Strategy To Engange Stakeholder
Industry partners of skilling programs	High	High	Helps them meet their CSR agenda Provides trained manpower for their operations/ industry	Give feedback on current industry skill requirements. Provide lab equipment, Training materials, Curriculum. Provide on-the-job training and placement support	Not be proactive.	Constant dialogue and communication Ensure proper credit for partnership Involvement in various steps of training process.

Annexure 4

Sample In-house SROI Working for A CSR Intervention Of XXX Company

Introduction

XXX Company, as part of its CSR, undertakes skill training for school and college dropout youth from underprivileged families, to help them enter a vocation and earn a livelihood. The trainees settle in either wage employment or set up their own micro-enterprises. Till date, over 25,000 youth have been trained.

Stakeholders to Skill Training

Skill training involves and impacts a variety of stakeholders and hence has both 'direct' and 'indirect' returns on the investment made towards training. While there are many stakeholders, the primary ones considered here are the youth, their family, the employer, society, and the nation.

Outcomes for Stakeholders and Establishing Materiality

No.	Stakeholder	Outcome	Can 'materiality be established'?
1.	Trainee	Increase in employment potential	Yes
		Income increase	Yes
		Increase in self-confidence, self-esteem, etc.	Likely, but difficult to assign materiality to this factor alone.
		Increased contribution to family sustenance and standard of living	Likely, but difficult to assign materiality to this factor alone
2.	Family	Decrease in spending on one individual	Yes
		Contribution to family sustenance and standard of living	Difficult to assign materiality to this factor alone

No.	Stakeholder	Outcome	Financial Proxy	Financial Value
1.	Trainee	Increase in employment potential	Cost if paying at commercial establishment to undergo this course	One time: Rs 25,000

No.	Stakeholder	Outcome	Financial Proxy	Financial Value
		Income increase	Salary per month @ Rs 9,000 and 10 per cent increase every year	1st year Rs 1,08,000 2nd year Rs 1,20,000 3rd year Rs 1,32,000 4th year Rs 1,44,000 5th year Rs 1,56,000 **TOTAL Rs 6,60,000**
2.	Family	Decrease in spending on one individual	Monthly decrease in spend on one individual or cost borne by the individual through his/her contribution out of income after training	1st year Rs 1,20,000 (@ 1,000 per month) 2nd year Rs 15,000 (@ 1,250 per month) 3rd year Rs 18,000 (@ 1,500 per month) 4th year Rs 21,000 (@ 1,750 per month) 5th year Rs 24,000 (@ 2,000 per month) TOTAL Rs 90,000
3.	Employer	Access to trained manpower	Cost of skilling a fresh person to that level	Rs 5,000 x 6 months = Rs 30,000

No.	Stakeholder	Outcome	Can 'materiality be established'?
3.	Employer	Access to trained manpower	Yes
4.	Society	Better family income leading to better-off society	Difficult to measure and hence difficult to assign materiality
		Employed and engaged individuals leading to a more peaceful and purposeful society	
5.	Nation	Higher GDP	Difficult to measure and hence difficult to assign materiality
		Higher taxes after a period of time	

- Sensitivity Analysis: Involves four main factors to be deducted (for other possibilities that exist in the system influencing the outcomes) from the financial values calculated.
- Deadweight: Part of the outcome that would have happened even without the intervention.
- Displacement: If the intervention has displaced any other similar opportunity or outcome.
- Attribution: If the outcomes of the intervention can be attributed to other factors in ecosystem.
- Drop-off: Time duration or period during or after which outcomes cannot necessarily be attributed to this intervention, or percentages with which the outcome from the intervention slowly tapers off.

Stakeholder	Outcome	Financial Proxy	Financial Value	Deadweight	Displacement	Attribution	Drop-off	Final Value
Trainee	Increase in employment potential	Cost of undergoing similar course	Rs 25,000		25%			**Rs 18,750**
	Income increase	Salary for five years	Rs 6,60,000	25%			20%	**Rs 363,000**
Family	Decrease in spending on one individual	Less spend on one individual by family	Rs 90,000	25%		25%		**Rs 45,000**
Employer	Access to trained manpower	Cost of skilling a fresh person to that level	Rs 30,000	30%				**Rs 21,000**
	TOTAL							**4,47,750**

Social Return on Investment

- Total expenditure on a trainee = Rs 15,000
- Total value created by intervention = Rs 4,47,750
- Social value created by intervention
- = Rs 4,47,750 – Rs 15,000 = Rs 4,32,750
- SROI ratio = Total value created by intervention/Total investment made
- SROI ratio for skill training = 4,47,750/15,000 = 29.85
- Social value created by skilling by the company
- With the assumptions and sensitivity analysis made, it can be concluded that for every rupee spent on skill training of an individual by the company, a social value of Rs 29.85 was created.

Bibliography

Ah-hen, C. (2016). 'Mauritius Corporate Social Responsibility—A Supplement to Social Protection System'. Paper. Braamfontein, Johannesburg: ASPEC and FES International Conference. www.saspen.org/conferences/comprehensive2016/SASPEN2016_Poster

Andriof, J., S. Waddock, B. Husted, and S.S. Rahman (2002). *Unfolding stakeholder thinking: theory, responsibility and engagement*. Sheffield: Greenleaf Publishing.

Armstrong, J. Scott (1977). 'Social Irresponsibility in Management'. *Journal of Business Research* 5, no. 3 (September): 185–213.

Arora, B., and R. Puranik (2004). 'A review of corporate social responsibility in India'. *Development* 47, no. 3: 93–100.

Bain and Co., and Dasra. *India Philanthropy Report 2022*.

Boggan, S. (2001). '"We Blew It": Nike Admits to Mistakes Over Child Labor.' *The Independent*, 20 October; reproduced in Common Dreams; https://www.commondreams.org/

Bowen, H.R. (1953). *Social Responsibilities of the Businessman.* New York: Harper & Brothers.

Carroll, A.B. (1979). 'Three-Dimensional Conceptual Model of Corporate Performance'. *The Academy of Management Review* 4, no. 4 (October): 497–505.

Carroll, A.B. (2008). 'A History of Corporate Social Responsibility: Concept and Practices'. In *The Oxford Handbook of Corporate Social Responsibility*, A. Crane et al. (eds). Oxford: Oxford University Press.

Chandler, D. (2019). *Strategic Corporate Social Responsibility: Sustainable Value Creation.* Fifth edition. Thousand Oaks, CA: Sage Publications.

Collins, C., and H. Flannery (2016). *When Billionaires Dominate Philanthropy.* Institute for Policy Studies, 21 November. https://ips-dc.org/billionaires-dominate-philanthropy/

Dahlsrud, A. (2006). 'How corporate social responsibility is defined: an analysis of 37 definitions'. *Corporate Social Responsibility and Environmental Management* 15: 1–13. https://doi.org/10.1002/csr.132

Deodhar, S.Y. (2015). *India's mandatory CSR, process of compliance and channels of spending.* Working Paper No. 2015-05-01. Ahmedabad: Indian Institute of Management.

Department for International Developement (2003). 'Tools for Development: A handbook for those engaged in development activity Performance and Effectiveness Department'. Department for International Development (DFID). March.

Ellen McArthur Foundation (n.d). 'Circular Economy Introduction'. https://ellenmacarthurfoundation.org/topics/circular-economy-introduction/overview

Emerson, J. (2010). 'Blended Value'. In *International Encyclopedia of Civil Society*, H.K. Anheier, and S. Toepler (eds). New York: Springer.

Examples of Enlightened Self-interest in Business. (2021, March 2). *Chron*. https://smallbusiness.chron.com

Frankental, P. (2001). 'Corporate social responsibility: a PR invention?'. *Corporate Communications: An International Journal* 6, no. 1: 18–23.

Frederick, W.C. (1960). 'The Growing Concern over Business Responsibility'. *California Management Review* 2, no. 4: 54–61. doi:10.2307/41165405

Frederick, W.C., J. Post, and K.E. Davis (1992). *Business and Society. Corporate Strategy, Public Policy, Ethics*. Seventh edition. London: McGraw-Hill.

Friedman, M. (1970). 'A Friedman doctrine—A Social Responsibility of Business is to Increase its Profits'. *The New York Times*, 13 September. https://www.nytimes.com/1970/09/13/archives/

Gandhi, M.K. (1942). *Harijan*. 22 February. Ahmedabad: Navjivan Press.

Gangopadhyay, S. (2014). 'CSR, out of the box: Mandated corporate social responsibility hurts shareholders, not firms'. *Business Standard*, 21 March. https://www.business-standard.com/article/opinion/

Hanlon, G., and P. Fleming (2009). 'Updating the Critical Perspective on Corporate Social Responsibility'. *Sociology Compass* 3, no. 6: 937–48.

Hayes, A. (2020). 'Corporate Citzenship'. Investopedia, 21 August. https://www.investopedia.com/terms/c/corporatecitizenship.asp

ICAI (2020). *Handbook on Audit of CSR Activities*. New Delhi: The Institute of Chartered Accountants of India. https://resource.cdn.icai.org/62737handbook-on-audit-of-csr-activities.pdf

IEG (n.d.). 'What is Monitoring and Evaluation?' Independent Evaluation Group. https://ieg.worldbankgroup.org/what-monitoring-and-evaluation

Jones, G. (2018). *Varieties of Green Business: Industries, Nations and Time*. Cheltenham (UK): Edward Elgar Publishing Ltd.

Jones, T.M. (1980). 'Corporate social responsibility revisited, redefined'. *California Management Review* 22, no. 3: 59–67.

Karnani, A. (2013). 'Mandatory CSR in India: A Bad Proposal.' *Stanford Social Innovation Review,* 20 May. https://ssir.org/articles/

Kotchen, M., and J. Moon (2012). 'Corporate Social Responsibility for Irresponsibility'. *The B.E. Journal of Economic Analysis & Policy (Contributions)* 12, no.1.

Lala, R.M. (2011). *The Art of Effective Giving*. Gurugram: HarperCollins India.

Lawlor, E., E. Neitzert, J. Nicholls, and T. Goodspeed (2009). *A Guide to Social Return on Investment*. London: New Economics Foundation. https://neweconomics.org/

Levitt, T. (1958). 'The dangers of social responsibility'. *Harvard Business Review*, 36 (September–October): 41–50.

Lin-Hi, N., and K. Müller. (2013). 'The CSR bottom line: Preventing corporate social irresponsibility'. *Journal of Business Research* 66, no. 10: 1928–36.

Lyon, T.P., and J.M. Maxwell (2011). 'Greenwash: Corporate Environmental Disclosure under Threat of Audit'. *Journal of Economics and Management Strategy* 20, no. 1: 3–41. https://doi.org/10.1111/j.1530-9134.2010.00282.x

Madhavan, N. (2011). 'TVS group has never faced a labour problem'. *Business Today.* 12 June. https://www.businesstoday.in/magazine/case-study/story/

Mehta, M. (2019). 'Ahmedabad's textile mill owners and workers both rallied around Gandhi on his return from South Africa'. *National Herald*, 8 October. https://www.nationalheraldindia.com/

Michael, B. (2003). 'Corporate social responsibility in international development: an overview and critique.' *Corporate Social Responsibility and Environmental Management* 10, no. 3 (September): 115–28. Wiley Online Library. DOI: 10.1002/csr.041

Ministry of Corporate Affairs (n.d.). *FAQ On CSR Cell*. https://www.mca.gov.in/MinistryV2/faq+on+csr+cell.html

———(2009). *Corporate Social Responsibility Voluntary Guidelines*. New Delhi: Government of India.

———(2011). *National Voluntary Guidelines on Social, Environmental and Economic Responsibilities of Business*. New Delhi: Government of India. https://www.mca.gov.in/Ministry/latestnews/National_Voluntary_Guidelines_2011_12jul2011.pdf

———(2014). 'Subject: Clarifications with regard to provisions of Corporate Social Responsibility under section 135 of the Companies Act, 2013'. General Circular No. 21/2014 No. 05/01/2014- CSR. New Delhi: Government of India. https://www.mca.gov.in/Ministry/pdf/General_Circular_21_2014.pdf

———(2019). *National Guidelines for Responsible Business Conduct*. New Delhi: Government of India. https://www.mca.gov.in/Ministry/pdf/NationalGuildeline_15032019.pdf]

———(2020) 'Subject: COVID-19 related Frequently Asked Questions (FAQs) on Corporate Social Responsibility (CSR)'. General Circular No. 15 /2020. F. No. CSR-01/4/2020-CSR

MCA. New Delhi: Government of India. https://www.mca.gov.in/Ministry/pdf/Notification_10042020.pdf

———(2021). 'Subject: Frequently Asked Questions (FAQs) on Corporate Social Responsibility (CSR) -reg'. General Circular No. 14/2021 E-file no.CSR-05/01/2021-CSR-MCA. New Delhi: Government of India. https://www.mca.gov.in/Ministry/pdf/FAQ_CSR.pdf

———(2021a). Companies (Corporate Social Responsibility Policy) Amendment Rules, 2021 'Notification.' *The Gazette of India*, 22 January. https://www.mca.gov.in/Ministry/pdf/CSRAmendmentRules_23012021.pdf

Ministry of Law and Justice.

Mitra, N., and R. Schmidpeter (2016). 'The Why, What and How of the CSR Mandate: The India Story'. In *Corporate Social Responsibility in India: Case and Developments After the Legal Mandate,* N. Mitra and R. Schmidpeter (eds). Switzerland: Springer International Publishing.

Moily, V. (2012). *First National CSR Conclave.* New Delhi: Indian Institute of Corporate Affairs. http://iica.in/images/synopsis_of_1st_CSR_Conclave.pdf

OECD (n.d). 'What is Impact Assessment?' https://www.oecd.org/sti/inno/ Porter, M.E., and M.R. Kramer (2006). 'Strategy and Society: The Link Between Competitive Advantage and Corporate Social Responsibility'. *Harvard Business Review*, December. https://hbr.org/2006/12/

———(2011). 'Creating Shared Value: How to reinvent capitalism—and unleash a wave of innovation and growth'. *Harvard Business Review* 89, Nos. 1 and 2, (January–February): 2–17. https://hbr.org/2011/01/

Praxis, Oxfam India, and Corporate Responsibility Watch (2018). 'Making Growth Inclusive: Analysing Inclusive Policies, Disclosures and Mechanisms of Top 100

Companies'. Disclosure Matters Series: Part V. https://www.corporatewatch.in/

PricewaterhouseCoopers Pvt. Ltd. (2013). *Handbook on Corporate Social Responsibility in India*. https://www.pwc.in/

Raghunathan, M.L. (2017) 'Corporate Social Responsibility in India—Pathways toward 2014, and Beyond'. *Amity Journal of Corporate Governance* 2, no. 1: 18–37.

Rai, S., Bansal, S. 2014. 'An analysis of corporate social responsibility expenditure in India', *Economic and Political Weekly*. Vol. XLIX (50).

Rai, S., Bansal, S. 2015. 'Factors Explaining Corporate Social Responsibility Expenditure in India', *Review of Market Integration*. Vol. 7(1).

Rangan, V.K., L. Chase, and S. Karim (2015). 'The Truth About CSR'. *Harvard Business Review* 93, nos. 1 and 2 (January–February): 40–49. https://hbr.org/2015/01/

Rietbergen-McCracken, J., and D. Narayan (Compiled) (1998). Participation and Social Assessment: Tools and Techniques. The World Bank. Washington.

Samhita (2016). 'Transforming India: The CSR Opportunity'. https://www.samhita.org/wp-content/uploads/2016/10/Transforming-India_-The-CSR-Opportunity.pdf

Sarkar, J., and S. Sarkar (2015). 'Corporate social responsibility in India: An effort to bridge the welfare gap'. (WP-2015-023). Mumbai: Indira Gandhi Institute of Development Research. http://www.igidr.ac.in/pdf/publication/

SEBI (2020). 'Working Group Report on Social Stock Exchange'. Committee Reports. Mumbai: Securities and Exchange Board of India. https://www.sebi.gov.in/reports-and-statistics/reports/jun-2020/

Shared Value Initiative Hong Kong (n.d.). 'What is Creating Shared Value?'. https://sharedvaluehk.org/what-is-creating-shared-value/

Sidel, M. (2000). 'New economy philanthropy in the high technology communities of Bangalore and Hyderabad, India: Partnership with thc state and the ambiguous search for social innovation'. Unpublished paper presented at Philanthropy and the City: A Historical Overview, New York. www.rockarch.org/publications/conferences/philcity.php

Singh, A., and P. Verma (2014). 'From Philanthropy to Mandatory CSR: A Journey Towards Mandatory Corporate Social Responsibility in India'. *International Journal of Business and Management Invention* 3, no. 8: 72–78.

Singh, J.V. (2010). 'Corporate Affairs Secretary R. Bandyopadhyay: "CSR Is Not Charity—It's a Win-Win Situation'. Knowledge@Wharton, 17 June. https://knowledge.wharton.upenn.edu/article/ Social Change UK. *An introduction to Social Return on Investment.* https://social-change.co.uk/

Sundar, P. (2000). *Beyond business: From merchant charity to corporate citizenship Indian business philanthropy through the ages.* New Delhi: Tata McGraw-Hill Publishing.

The SROI Network (2016). *Guide to commissioning for maximum value.* http://www.socialvalueuk.org/

The SROI Network (2012). *A Guide to Social Return on Investment.* http://www.socialvaluelab.org.uk/

UK Aid Connect (n.d.). *Guidance Note: Developing a Theory of Change.* https://assets.publishing.service.gov.uk/media/

UNDG (2011). *Results-Based Management Handbook: Harmonizing RBM concepts and approaches for improved development results at country level.* New York: United

Nations Sustainable Development Group. [Formerly, the United Nations Development Group (UNDG)] https://unsdg.un.org/

United Nations Global Compact (2004). *The Global Compact Leaders Summit, Final Report*. New York: United Nations.

Vishwanathan, P., H.J. van Oosterhout, P.P.M.A.R. Heugens, and M. van Essen (2020). 'Strategic CSR: A Concept Building Meta-Analysis'. *Journal of Management Studies* 57, no. 2 (March): 314–50. [First published: 21 May 2019]. https://doi.org/10.1111/joms.12514

Watkins, R., M. West Meiers, and Y.L. Visser (2012). *A Guide to Assessing Needs: Essential Tools for Collecting Information, Making Decisions, and Achieving Development Results*. Washington DC: World Bank. https://openknowledge.worldbank.org/

Werther, B.W., and D. Chandler (2011). *Strategic Corporate Social Responsibility: Stakeholders in a Global Environment*. Los Angeles: Sage.

Williams, T. (n.d.). 'Corporate citizenship: Your company's role in society'. *Economist Education*. https://execed.economist.com/

World Bank (n.d.). 'Toolkit for Monitoring and Evaluation of Agricultural Water Management Projects'. Washington DC: Agricultural and Rural Development Department, World Bank. https://documents1.worldbank.org/

World Business Council for Sustainable Development (2008)

WEBSITES

https:www.aai.aero/

https://www.amul.com/

https:// azimpremjifoundation.org

https://www.bcorporation.net
https://bits-pilani.ac.in/bitsFactsHistory
https://www.bridgespan.org/locations/bridgespan-india/pay-what-it-takes-india#:
https://www.coalindia.in
https://www corporatefinanceinstitute.com
https://credibilityalliance.org/
https://www.crisil.com/en/home/our-businesses/sme-solutions/corporate-responsibility/voluntary-organisation.html
https://www.crisil.com/en/home/newsroom/press-releases/2019/10/crisil-foundation-bags-national-csr-award
https://csrbox.org/
https://csrbox.org/India_CSR_Project_Mahindra-&-Mahindra-Ltd-Integrated-Watershed-Management-Program-Madhya-Pradesh
https://csrxchange.gov.in/
https://dpe.gov.in/dpe-guidelines/corporate-social-responsibility
https://ec.europa.eu/info/sites/default/files/recommendations-subgroup-corporate-social-responsibility_en.pdf
https://economictimes.indiatimes.com/news/company/corporate-trends/view-is-india-esg-ready-firms-seems-to-be-getting-serious-about-it. 20.4.22.
https://economictimes.indiatimes.com/news/company/corporate-trends/parliament-panel-seeks-constituency-wise-csr-spending-by-top-10-companies. 28.3.22.
https:// www.ftserussell.com
https://www.gdrc.org/ngo/logical-fa.pdf
https://www.giveindia.org/
https://www.globalgiving.org/
https://www.globalreporting.org/how-to-use-the-gri-standards/
https://goodera.com/in/

https:www.hclfoundation.org
https://www.gov.uk/government/publications/dfid-how-to-note-guidance-on-using-the-revised-logical-framework
https://www.gstlegal.co.in/admin/legal_upload_files/
https://www.guidestar.org/
https://www.ifc.org
https://www. iica.nic.in
https://iica.nic.in/nfcsr_about.aspx
https://indiacsr.in/
https://www.iocl.com/aboutus/Awards-and- Recognitions.aspx
https://www.iso.org/
https://www.ivolunteer.in/about-ivolunteer
https://ivolunteerawards.com/winners-2020/
https://www.jamnalalbajajfoundation.org/jamnalal-bajaj/about
https://www.johnelkington.com/archive/TBL
https://www.livingmypromise.org/
https://www.mca.gov.in/content/mca/global/en/acts rules/ebooks/#Corporate_Social_Responsibility
https://www.mca.gov.in/MCA21/
https://www.muhammadyunus.org/
https://www://mof.govmu.org/
https://www.nanhikali.org/
https://www.nationalcsrnetwork.in/
https:// ngodarpan.gov.in
https://www. nirdpr.org.in
https://www.nmdc.co.in
https://www. nseindia.com
https:// www.oecd.org
https://ongcindia.com
http://www.paranjapeautocast.com/csr.html
https://www.povertyactionlab.org/sites/default/files/
https://www.powergrid.in/csr/key-csr-activities

https://www.samhita.org/
https://www.sasb.org
https:/// www.sattva.co.in/
https://www.sdgimpact.undp.org
https://www.sebi.gov.in
https://www.sparkminda.com/csrminda/
https://sswm.info/sites/default/files/reference_attachments/ODA.
https://www. Sasb
sustainabledevelopment.un.org/content/documents/5987our-common-future.pdf
https://www.tatasteel.com/media/6085/ jamshedpur-brochure.pdf
https://www.tata.com
https://www. thegiin.org
https://www.tiss.edu
https://www.undp.org
https://www.unido.org
https://www.wbcsd.org/
https:// www.who.int/
https:// worldbank.org/

Index

Acknowledgements

'Behind every lazy writer is a nagging husband' could be the story of my life. It is to Raghu that I owe all thanks for coaxing, cajoling, pushing and scolding me into writing this book after a long hiatus from writing anything apart from my blog. And for setting an example of how to be disciplined about writing, thanks to which I finished the first draft in three months.

This was a project taken up and completed at the height of COVID lockdowns. Less distraction definitely makes for more words per day! But even more importantly, COVID opened up immense learning opportunities. I could take part in several amazing webinars, workshops, training programmes and conferences that I would not possibly have been able to attend otherwise. And what I learned through these, whether as a speaker or a listener, helped me sharpen my perspectives and expand my knowledge. Thanks to the organizers of all these, as well as the speakers and participants.

Thanks to Mamata Pandya and Avanish Kumar, who are always there to help—whether it is inputs on content, in editing, or for general encouragement. To Savithri for her 360 degree support, and Harini for tech-gyan. Good to have friends who have your back.

I am also beholden to the Centre for Environment Education, where I spent close to two decades. It provided the most intellectually stimulating and happy work environment ever. It is thanks to CEE that I am the professional and person I am.

To GMR Varalakshmi Foundation where I worked for fifteen years, I owe my gratitude for the opportunity to understand and practice CSR.

Thanks to my colleagues at 226, for being part of my learning-journey. And to CSW colleagues—some of the tables and annexures in the book owe a lot to them.

I must thank Krishan Chopra the then-Editor of Harper Collins, for seeing the potential of the book and taking it on, and Sachin Sharma, who patiently worked with me through the various stages of getting the book out.

To Saroj, Manju, and Barnalee for being part of the family.

To my parents and mother-in-law, who would have been so happy and proud.

About the Author

Meena Raghunathan was executive director, CSR, at GMR Varalakshmi Foundation, where she set up and managed the CSR function for the GMR Group. Prior to that, she worked at the Centre for Environment Education, on national and international projects related to education, training and communication to support sustainable development.

She has to her credit college and school textbooks, books for children and young people, policy papers, publications for educators, etc., and is a blogger. Meena serves on corporate and non-profit Boards, as well as Boards of educational and skilling institutions. She is an advisor on CSR, ESG, skilling and education for sustainable development, and also teaches these.